Artisanal
PRESERVES

SMALL-BATCH *jams, jellies, marmalades,* AND MORE

❧

Madelaine Bullwinkel

A SURREY BOOK

AGATE

CHICAGO

The first Surrey Books edition of this book was published as *Gourmet Preserves Chez Madelaine* in 2005. This edition has been revised and redesigned.

Artisanal Preserves
ISBN 13: 978-1-57284-341-7
ISBN 10: 1-57284-341-1
ebook ISBN 13: 978-1-57284-889-4
ebook ISBN 10: 1-57284-889-8

Printed in the United States

The Library of Congress has cataloged a previous edition of this book as follows:

Bullwinkel. Madelaine.
Gourmet preserves Chez Madelaine 1 delicious marmalades, jams, jellies, and preserves to make at home—plus easy muffins, scones, crêpes, puddings, pastries, desserts, and breakfast treats to serve with them / Madelaine Bullwinkel. —1st ed.
p. cm.
Includes index.
ISBN 1-57284-078-1
I. Jam. a. Jelly. I. Title.
TX612.J3B8523 2005
641.8'52—dc22
2004028507

10 9 8 7 6 5 4 3 2 1   24 25 26 27 28

Surrey Books is an imprint of Agate Publishing. Agate books are available in bulk at discount prices. For more information, visit agatepublishing.com.

For my Mother, Mary Gaylord de Huszar, and George

Contents

Introduction

THERE ARE SEVERAL REASONS WHY this small cookbook on fruit preserving remains in print after forty years. *Artisanal Preserves* is a teaching tool, a shop manual for those making fruit preserves for the first time. The different kinds of preserves are defined, techniques are explained, equipment recommendations are made. Each chapter follows a given technique with step-by-step directions.

An artisanal awareness of the "whys" of preserving in addition to these "how-tos" sets this book apart. It begins with a description of the pectin jell in layman's terms that is then applied to recipes for each kind of preserve. With this understanding, home cooks can guide rather than simply follow the preserving process.

Other features unique to *Artisanal Preserves* are its bread and dessert chapters. It was my intention from the beginning to encourage preservers to showcase their flavorful jams and jellies at mealtime and when entertaining.

What's new this time? The fourth edition of *Artisanal Preserves* introduces apple jelly as the artisan's alternative to commercial pectin products. This shelf-stable jelly replaces apple pectin stock and the use of commercial pectin in previous editions. Apple jelly is a complete pectin source for wine and vegetable jellies as well as preserves made with low-pectin fruit.

I have also added new material to the chapter on the history of preserving. After all, preserving is a practice that evolved over millennia and was once essential to our survival. Today, fruit preserving continues to support a healthy lifestyle and satisfy a need to work with our hands.

For the first time, all preserves are vacuum sealed in a boiling water bath in keeping with USDA standards. I have abandoned my practice of inverting freshly filled jars to create a quick vacuum seal. This method no longer consistently protects preserves from spoilage in our warming environment.

While safe to store for long periods, a fruit preserve tastes best when eaten before next year's crop arrives. Small jars of homemade preserves make great gifts to thank some-one, build friendships, and show appreciation. I keep a supply of quarter-pint jars on hand to gift to someone at a moment's notice. Those who think to return an empty jar are rewarded with a freshly filled one.

Now it's time for you to join in the delight and satisfaction of creating delicious fruit preserves in your own kitchen. Feel free to contact me with stories of your success and questions should you have setbacks. I will be happy to respond at chezm@chezm.com.

CHAPTER

1

A

Short History

OF PRESERVING

THE FIRST PRESERVES

Since prehistoric times, human survival has depended on the ability to preserve abundant harvests for periods when food was scarce. Early man devised ways to avoid spoilage of plants and animal meat by freezing, drying, salting, or fermenting them. Honey was the sweetener used by the Greeks and Romans to preserve fruit and meat.

The first description of fruit preserved with cane sugar is found in The Decameron, a collection of stories written by the fourteenth-century Italian writer Giovanni Boccaccio. Ten aristocratic young Florentines are described spooning fruit preserves into their pampered mouths as they live in luxury, isolated from the plague that ravages their hometown. At that time, sugar was an expensive import from the Near East, having arrived in Venice before the twelfth century. Its use spread into Europe, but it remained a precious commodity until the eighteenth century.

THE SEARCH FOR CHEAP SUGAR

By the middle of the sixteenth century, translations of Italian cookbooks with recipes for preserves began to appear in France. The first instance of a marmalet in an English cookbook also dates from the early 1500s. Its source is a Portuguese recipe for preserved marmelo quince. Sweet preserves graced the royal tables of Europe with increasing regularity as their popularity spread northward.

When agriculture developed on the North American continent, sugar cane became a staple crop to export to Europe. Before the Civil War, good-sized sugar plantations existed in Louisiana, Alabama, Florida, Georgia, and Mississippi, and many Caribbean islands grew sugar crops using slave labor. When the demand for sugar in America outgrew homegrown supplies, cheap molasses was imported from the islands.

In the middle of the nineteenth century, an inexpensive method for processing cane sugar was perfected. On the heels of this discovery came the large-scale production of sugar extracted from beets. Now American households could afford to make fruit preserves.

THE VACUUM SEAL: A TIMELESS INVENTION

In 1810, a French candy maker, Nicholas Appert, invented a method for sealing food in glass jars. But it took another century and the ingenuity of three Americans to create a vacuum-sealed jar for the home cook in America. John Mason was the first to patent a glass jar with a threaded top and airtight metal cap in 1858. When Mason's patents expired, the Ball brothers began producing Mason jars. In 1915, John Kerr bought the rights to a German heat-sealing gasket on a lacquered metal lid that would vent air when heated and then seal quickly when cooled. Today we buy Ball's version of the Mason jar with a Kerr heat-sealing lid and screw cap.

This pioneering innovation coupled with the drop in sugar prices had a dramatic effect in the marketplace. It made homemade preserves more accessible and led to the safe, inexpensive manufacture of preserves on an industrial scale. More and more people took advantage of the opportunity to purchase preserves, while homemade preserves continued to be a staple in rural communities and among those who carried on family cooking traditions. The gap between the flavor and healthfulness of small-batch home preserving and their supermarket counterparts has increasingly widened with widespread industrial use of corn sweeteners and chemical stabilizers.

PRESERVING TRENDS

The isolation of pectin, the fibrous jelling agent in fruit, is a relatively recent discovery, made by the French chemist Henri Braconnet in 1825. One hundred years later, powdered pectin extracted from citrus fruit was introduced in the American marketplace. Use of concentrated pectin gave homemakers a foolproof way to make firmly jelled fruit preserves if they were willing to add more sugar by weight than fruit to their preserve.

The fact that Certo and Sure-Jell pectins are now sold in a variety of concentrations testifies to the awareness that these products create overly sweet jellies and preserves. In 1980, Pomona Universal Pectin began selling a sugar-free, preservative-free citrus powder that activates the jell with the addition of a calcium solution. This jelling method allows sugar or its substitutes to be added at will, but limits the cook to Pomona's recipe. This jell breaks down with longer cooking times than one or two minutes. All industrial pectins limit the preserver to a formula that prioritizes the jell at the expense of natural fruit flavor.

In 1974, the sale of glass jars by the Ball Corporation rose dramatically. The people who had returned to home gardening in the early 1970s were learning to preserve their fruits and vegetables for the winter. The rise in preserving at home was symptomatic of a period of national self-scrutiny in America. We questioned the quality of our air and water, the use of pesticides in farming, and the presence of additives and chemical preservatives in processed foods.

The rise of sustainable and organic farming practices attests to America's continuing commitment to combat the deterioration of our environment and food supply. The number of organic fruits and vegetables available at the grocery has proliferated, as have local farmers' markets. This growth demonstrates a desire for local, small-scale farming. Making fruit preserves serves this artisanal spirit and the drive to elevate our quality of life at the table.

CHAPTER

2

Techniques
AND
Equipment
FOR PRESERVING

W HETHER YOU'RE NEW TO FRUIT PRESERVING or a veteran, this chapter is an essential review of basic definitions and a brisk walk-through of the process itself. There is a reassuring amount of ritual activity in preserving and some fascinating kitchen chemistry at work. We will explain the "whys" that underlie the "how-to's" of preserving because they help you make better decisions as you cook. Once you've mastered pectin jell chemistry, you can experiment with confidence.

DEFINITIONS OF JAM, JELLY, MARMALADE, AND PRESERVES

All the recipes in this book, aside from the baking and dessert chapters, are fruit preserves. Almost always, fruit is cooked with sugar to preserve its flavor and prevent spoilage. Our one exception is no-sugar jam, which relies simply on the fructose that is naturally present in fruit.

Several kinds of preserves rely on the jell:

- Jellies are jelled high-pectin fruit juices.
- Preserves are fruit pieces suspended in a fruit-juice jell.
- Marmalades are citrus fruits and peels jelled in their own juices.

A jam is simply fruit cooked with sugar and lemon juice until it thickens to a spreadable consistency. This is the ideal technique for preserving low-pectin fruits. An adventurous cook can experiment with unusual fruit combinations and the addition of herbs and spices. A jam made with a high-pectin fruit will sometimes jell but still remain a jam because it lacks saturated fruit pieces. It is also possible to make a jam without sugar. The combination of unsweetened fruit juices with fruits and berries or dried fruit can create satisfying sweetness and texture in no-sugar jams.

WHAT IS PECTIN AND HOW DOES IT FORM A JELL?

Pectin is a fibrous carbohydrate, bulging with entrapped water molecules. All fruits contain pectin when unripe, and many retain some pectin when ripe while others

THE DIGITAL SCALE

Weighing fruits and berries is much easier with a digital scale. The footprint on the counter of this handy tool is that of a small notebook. Countertop scales are accurate to a fraction of an ounce and can convert ounces into grams. Best of all, there is a reset button that compensates for the weight of a strainer or measuring cup and allows the cook to weigh only the contents. It's the most efficient way to weigh both small quantities of loose berries and large fruits.

retain very little. High levels of pectin are found in apples, black and red currants, cranberries, blackberries, blueberries, and quinces. The citrus fruits—orange, grapefruit, lemon, and lime—carry pectin in the white portion of their bitter peels. They are considered to have a good pectin level, as do Concord grapes, plums, red raspberries, and strawberries. Fruits with low or negligible pectin content include apricots, cherries, figs, pears, peaches, pineapple, and rhubarb.

Fruit has to be simmered for 10 minutes before it releases its pectin. When a little acid is present in this heated solution, the molecular structure and physical properties of pectin will change. It becomes less possessive of its water and more attracted to other pectin molecules.

The addition of sugar at this point causes a chemical reaction. In the presence of heat and acid, granulated sugar breaks down to its simpler forms: glucose and fructose. These sugars hungrily strip water molecules off the pectin chains. The unfettered pectin strands then come together freely. This dense web of pectin that holds and supports the aqueous sugars is a jell.

HOW TO MEASURE THE PECTIN LEVEL IN FRUIT

Performing the pectin test is an optional exercise. Recipe ingredients in *Artisanal Preserves* have all been tested and measured to assure success. This pectin test is important only if you wish to experiment or reconfirm the pectin level. Nonetheless, curious cooks will find that measuring pectin fulfills the irresistible desire to actually see what is otherwise invisible in the saucepan. This measurement also ensures your control of the preserving process.

To perform the pectin test, measure 1 tablespoon of unsweetened, cooked fruit juice at room temperature onto a small plate. Stir in 1 to 1½ tablespoons of grain alcohol (available at liquor stores) or rubbing alcohol, and let this mixture stand for one minute before stirring it with the flattened tines of a fork. Pectin will appear as a translucent, gelatinous mass gathered on the tines or falling in thick strands from the fork. Small, scattered lumps or ripples of pectin that don't cling to the tines indicate a low pectin level. Reducing the juices or adding melted apple jelly will be needed to create a jell. (See illustration on page 12.)

Throw out the alcohol solution immediately after each test without tasting it. Grain alcohol is 90 percent alcohol and rubbing alcohol is toxic. They are also flammable and should be stored in a cool, dark place.

FRUITS WITH *High* PECTIN LEVELS	FRUITS WITH *Good* PECTIN LEVELS	FRUITS WITH *Low* PECTIN LEVELS
Blackberry	Grapefruit	Apricot
Black Currant	Lemon	Cherry
Black Raspberry	Lime	Fig
Blueberry	Orange	Kiwifruit
Concord Grape	Plum	Nectarine
Crabapple	Red Raspberry	Peach
Cranberry	Strawberry	Pear
Green Apple		Rhubarb
Quince		Pineapple
Red Currant		
Serviceberry		

MEASURING UTENSILS

Measuring utensils are calibrated for specific uses. Glass measures are designed to hold liquids while metal cups and spoons are sized for dry ingredients. The home preserver will want a collection of glass measures in pint, quart, and 2-quart sizes. A set of nesting metal cup measures and teaspoon to tablespoon measures are also essential.

HOW TO RAISE THE PECTIN LEVEL FOR THE JELL

Only fruits and berries with the highest pectin levels produce cooked juices with sufficient pectin to jell quickly. One easy strategy to improve the pectin level in a fruit juice is to include 25 percent underripe fruit. Underripe fruits and berries are also more acidic, a condition that acts as a catalyst in the jelling process.

Recipes that combine fruits with differing pectin levels, such as Peach and Raspberry Preserves (see page 142) and Citrus Marmalade with Apricots (see page 117), exemplify another way to raise pectin levels naturally. They also hint at the synergetic flavor potential of combined fruit flavors.

When the inclusion of underripe fruit or the addition of high-pectin fruit are not sufficient to produce the desired pectin level, the next alternative is to concentrate the pectin by reducing the volume. You will find that some recipes in the jelly chapter call for reducing fruit juices by as much as half their volume for this purpose.

In recipes for the most delicate wine jellies or quick-jelled preserves, none of the above techniques will be adequate to the task of producing a sufficient pectin level for the jell. The most natural alternative is to add homemade apple jelly. Apple jelly itself has a sweet, mild flavor that complements other fruits without asserting its own flavor. Several jelly recipes and "quick" preserve recipes use this technique. The jelly is first melted and then added in the same volume as the fruit juices or fruit pieces. It will cool to a soft-jell consistency.

TESTING FOR PECTIN

Stir 1 tablespoon of fruit juice into 1½ tablespoons of grain alcohol.

After 1 minute, pour the mixture onto a plate.

Connected strands indicate good pectin content. Reduce juices by one-half before adding sugar.

Coherent masses of pectin indicate excellent jelling potential. Use sugar cup-for-cup with juice.

MEASURING SUGAR AND ACID FOR THE JELL

High pectin fruit juices will jell when the same volume of sugar is added. The acid level is important to hasten this chemical reaction. I ask you to add 1 tablespoon of freshly squeezed lemon juice per cup of juice. A citrus juice also acts to complement and balance the preserve's sweetness. When the pectin level, sugar content, and lemon juice are in proper proportion, a jell forms in 5 to 10 minutes.

GETTING STARTED: STERILIZING PRESERVING JARS

Begin by bringing water to a boil in the large pot where the filled jars will be vacuum sealed. Sterilize the number of empty jars needed for the recipe at hand for 15 minutes while you prepare you preserves. *Note: The lids will be sterilized later, and the screw caps need only to be clean.*

At the same time, set aside a cooling rack near the range, first to drain the empty jars and then to hold filled jars. Set out new lids, screw caps for sealing the jars, and a clean towel. Other important pieces of equipment are a funnel for filling the jars without spillage and a thermometer to check the temperature as it cooks. Tongs, a jar lifter, and oven mitts are also necessities when handling the hot jars.

POTS FOR STERILIZING JARS

Select a large pot for sterilizing empty jars and vacuum-sealing all preserves. My preferred vessel is an aluminum pasta pot with a slotted insert that holds the jars off the bottom so they don't bounce around in the boiling water. A 12-quart stock pot that will accommodate a 10-inch round cake cooling rack is a good alternative.

CLEARING THE WATER

From time to time preserving jars will come out of the sterilizing pot with a gritty residue on their surface. This could be paper debris from a jar label or mineral build-up in the water. The addition of a tablespoon of distilled vinegar per quart of water will cause these materials to fall to the bottom and clear the water. Replace the water bath with fresh water at the next opportunity.

PREPARING FRUIT FOR PRESERVING

Each of the recipes specifies fruit quantities by the pound or, in the case of larger fruits, by the piece, and sometimes by both. Rinsing is all that is required for berries and soft fruits. Organic, hard, and citrus fruits receive a scrubbing with a vegetable brush as well as a rinsing in cold water in my kitchen.

The unwanted skin of apples and pears is easily removed with a peeler or paring knife. Blanching in boiling water is the preferred method for removing the skin of soft fruits such as apricots, peaches, and tomatoes. This process involves dipping the fruit in boiling water for 30 seconds, then immediately submerging it in an ice water bath to stop further cooking. When the fruit is cool enough to handle, the skin will slip off easily.

The peel of citrus fruits receives special attention because it is the source of high-quality pectin and fragrant oils. The outer colored portion contains fragrant oil that gives the fruit its characteristic aroma. The spongy, white inner portion is rich in pectin but is also quite bitter. Marmalade recipes will clearly specify whether or not the superficial zest, deep narrow strips, or a whole citrus peel will be used. In more delicate marmalades, a portion of the white inner peel is wrapped in cloth and simmered with the fruit mixture to extract its pectin. It is then squeezed and removed before sugar is added.

All fruits are sectioned, sliced, or chopped into pieces roughly the same size. This assures that preserves cook evenly and create a consistent texture. I prefer to chop up fruit by hand to achieve the right mouthfeel of the finished product. A mandoline or food-slicer is an alternative tool. The food processor is reserved for chopping hard fruits and unpeeled sections of citrus fruits.

KNIVES

A small collection of sharpened, high-quality knives makes fruit preparation a pleasurable task. A large chef's knife will aid in cutting up apples, pineapples, and citrus fruits. A paring knife is a more comfortable size when working with small fruits and berries. A finely serrated tomato knife gives the preserver excellent control when thinly slicing unpeeled citrus fruits and tough-skinned plums and tomatoes. If marmalade becomes your specialty, the purchase of a small bird's beak knife is advisable. It has a curved blade that cuts off the surface of a round fruit with a single flick of the wrist.

THE COOKING PROCESS

Despite the history and romance associated with a copper preserving pot, I prefer to prepare fruit preserves in modern non-reactive pots and pans, ranging in size from 4 to 8 quarts for small-batch preserving. I begin with the lid on the pot once the fruit is added and heat is turned on. It allows the mixture to come to the boil more quickly. Often a recipe will call for the addition of a small amount of water to coat the bottom of the pan and prevent soft fruit from sticking. Once the boil is reached, the lid is removed and the heat is turned down until the fruit mixture is gently simmering. All the fruits are then cooked at least 10 minutes undisturbed.

Lemon juice is added after this initial cooking period and before the sugar, which is stirred in, ½ cup at a time. The cook waits until the juices begin to boil again before adding the next half cup. In the jam recipes, simmering continues until the cook is satisfied with the preserve's consistency.

Preserves that jell take a slightly different course. The juice is separated from the fruit pulp after the initial cooking period, and sugar is added to the juices. They will boil up with a vigor that cannot be stirred down once the optimal amount of sugar and lemon juice are added. Insert a digital thermometer (see page 18) at this point.

The jell point on the thermometer is 8 degrees above the boiling temperature of water, which is 212°F at sea level. If you are

PANS FOR COOKING FRUIT PRESERVES

Select a heavy 5-quart saucepan with heatproof handles and lid for recipes that call for 2 pounds of fruit. An 8-quart pot is a more comfortable size for larger quantities and fruits that foam up when boiled. Preferred materials are coated aluminum or ceramic-covered cast iron. Stainless steel pans are acceptable if they have a heavy copper or nickel coating on the bottom to improve its conductivity.

Thin metal pans are poor preserving pans because they are vulnerable to burning the fragile fruit and sugar contents over the hot flame required for fruit preserving.

Uncoated aluminum pans are also discouraged as containers for fruit mixtures. The acidic character of preserves strips off aluminum oxide, a compound that forms naturally on untreated aluminum surfaces. Although it's not toxic, it is an undesirable ingredient in a fruit preserve. For that reason, all recipes in *Artisanal Preserves* call for non-reactive pans.

TOOLS FOR MARMALADE

One of three handy tools will be useful when removing the outer peel from citrus fruits for marmalades. The stripper tool has a single groove that gouges a deep narrow trough in the peel. The vegetable peeler—which comes in many designs—removes the thin outer skin and flesh of fruits. A zester has a row of tiny holes that scrape off the most superficial layer of skin on a citrus peel.

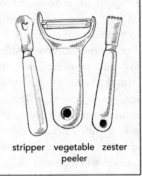

stripper   vegetable   zester
peeler

not at sea level, submerge the thermometer in the boiling water bath to determine the boiling point, then add 8 degrees to establish your specific jell point. (Test any new thermometer this way, even if you live at sea level. Thermometers are not always accurate.) If you're using a candy thermometer, hold it vertically and bend over to read the temperature at eye level. Your preserve will not jell until the exact temperature is reached.

ARE WE THERE YET? TESTING FOR THE JELL

When the candy thermometer reaches about 216°F, juices will begin to sheet off a spoon. To run this quick test, dip a large metal spoon in the bubbling preserve, fill it, then let the liquid pour off one side. If the juices collect together and fall in a single drop or in a sheet, the jelly is nearing the jell point. This is a reassuring but not a definitive sign of a jell.

The next test to run, when the thermometer reaches 218°F, involves a cold plate. (It helps to have planned ahead by placing a plate in the freezer.) Take the pan off the heat. Pour a teaspoon of hot liquid on the cold plate and return it to the freezer for a minute or two. Take the cold plate and tilt to see if the juice will hold its shape on the plate. Then, run your finger through the juice. If the smeared juice leaves a pattern of wrinkles in its wake, the preserve has reached the jell point.

A thermometer remains the best way to test for the fruit jell. For accuracy, test the thermometer when new as indicated in the section above. View the temperature column at eye level. For added insurance, continue cooking the preserve that has reached the jell point for one more minute.

ADDING HERBS, SPICES, AND LIQUORS TO PRESERVES

Once you gain confidence in your preserving skills, start adding fresh herbs, powdered spices, and liquors that add an imaginative touch to your preserves. You'll find examples in this book to show you when and how to add fresh thyme to grape jelly, cardamom to tart cherries, and Pernod to pears. All of these seasonings contain essential oils that are aromatic and therefore volatile.

Their ephemeral nature requires that herbs and some spices be added at the end of the cooking process. The herbs are not "cooked" but are submerged and steeped in the finished preserve for a few minutes before it is ladled into jars. Distilled liquor is added at the last minute, just long enough to drive off the alcohol. You can verify the strength of these additions by cooling a tablespoon of preserve quickly and tasting it. Add more seasoning and continue steeping or cooking if its presence is not discernable.

Some spices, on the other hand, have sturdy oils that become embedded in the complex aroma of fruit preserves during cooking. I advise adding cinnamon stick, star anise, and gingerroot early in the cooking process. Tie small spice pieces in cloth so they will be easy to retrieve at the end of the cooking process.

FILLING AND VACUUM SEALING IN A HOT WATER BATH

Once the jell point is reached, transfer the hot preserve to a large glass measure. Jellies may need skimming to remove surface foam that will mar their clarity once they

STRAINING JUICES

Line a conical sieve or strainer with a clean tea towel or fine mesh cloth to strain cooked fruit juices. If the cloth is new or not made specifically for kitchen use, wash it in mild soap to remove the sizing. Always rinse and squeeze dry the cloth before pouring juices through it.

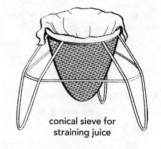

cheesecloth

conical sieve for straining juice

are poured into jars. Let fruit preserves and marmalades sit for 5 to 10 minutes and stir them occasionally to trap the fruit pieces evenly in the jell as the mixture cools.

You may take this opportunity to transfer the sterilized jars from their hot water bath to the cooling rack. Briefly submerge the new lids and let them drain on a clean towel nearby. This is a good time to submerge the plastic or metal funnel designed to fit inside the lip of the sterilized jars.

Fit the funnel into the mouth of the jar and pour the preserve to within ¼ inch of the lip. Thicker preserves with fruit pieces are better ladled into the jars to avoid

THERMOMETERS

The digital probe thermometer with a 500°F temperature range is an exacting and nearly instantaneous measuring device available in a wide range of prices. Its only drawback is its short measuring stem. The pan of preserves must be tilted to submerge enough of the stem to get an accurate reading. Even though this takes less than a minute, some may find their hands become uncomfortably warm.

A candy thermometer is the time-honored guide to measuring temperature. It can be left in the hot bubbling preserves, and some models clip to the side of the vessel, allowing for hands-free temperature reading. Do not confuse a candy with a deep-fry thermometer: the candy thermometer defines temperature in two-degree increments while the one for deep-frying is calibrated to read every five degrees.

More expensive, but well worth its price, is the Matfer Bourgeat Candy Thermometer. Its gauge is filled with red alcohol rather than mercury, and a metal cage protects both the thermometer and the cook. It's easy to use, safer than a standard candy thermometer, and equally accurate.

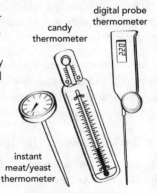

digital probe thermometer

candy thermometer

The instant meat/yeast thermometer with a temperature range of 0°F to 220°F is the least desirable choice for determining the temperature of preserves and baked goods. I would use it only if the other thermometers are not available.

instant meat/yeast thermometer

TESTING FOR JELL

Thermometer Test: Measure the temperature of water on your thermometer at boiling (212°F at sea level).

Spoon Test: Preserves will fall in a single sheet at 216°F.

Thermometer Test: Test for the jelling point by adding 8°F to the temperature reading on your thermometer at boiling (220°F at sea level).

Cold Plate Test: Jelly will wrinkle on a cold plate if it has jelled.

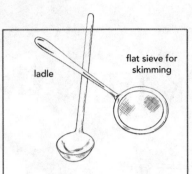

ladle

flat sieve for
skimming

SKIMMING AND FILLING

A flat, fine-mesh stainless steel strainer makes easy work of skimming foam from jellies and jams. It also comes in handy as a means of removing telltale pips that rise to the surface of simmering marmalades. A large spoon with a shallow bowl is an alternative skimming device.

For the job of transferring hot preserves from the glass measure to the preserving jar, select a ladle with a half-cup bowl. Use a wide-mouth plastic funnel to fill hot jars without spilling.

funnel

8 oz.
quilted jar

splattering. Lift the funnel to the next jar, then check the filled jar to make sure it is filled and no liquid has touched the rim of the lip. If this does occur, dip a paper towel in the recently boiled water and wipe the lip clean. Attach the new, sterilized lid and screw on the cap.

Once the jars are filled, submerge them in boiling water to cover by 1 to 2 inches as advised in the USDA's preserving guidelines. Take care to separate the jars in the bath. Maintain the boil for 10 minutes, then lift out the jars to cool on a rack. Tighten the screw cap, which will loosen when the lid vacuum seals the jar. Label and store after cooling.

Before the advent of vacuum sealing, the artisan preserver had to rely on fruit's natural acids and the preservative properties of sugar to protect against the growth of mold and bacteria. Even today, the best way to extend the shelf life of your preserves is to store them in a dark, cool place in your home. A cellar, basement, or lower kitchen cabinet away from appliances are excellent locations. But don't hoard your jams and jellies! They will taste best if eaten within six months. Make sure that each sealed jar has a label with the contents and date.

Occasionally, despite all precautions, a preserve will develop mold, a fermented odor, or a changed appearance during storage. Discard these jars immediately. It was once common practice to simply scrape the mold off the top of jelly and eat what lay beneath.

We now know these molds produce deep, invisible roots that carry mycotoxins that build up in the body over time. Follow the standard practice of refrigerating a vacuum-sealed jar after opening.

PRESERVE EXPERIMENTS

As you gain experience in following recipes, your ability to experiment will emerge. Over time, you will become adept at efficiently timing and artfully balancing tastes, textures, and scents in preserves. The recipes in *Artisanal Preserves* are as precise as I can make them. But once you are comfortable with your own skills, let the experiments begin.

In addition to practice, I would also add patience to the list of qualities important to a preserving pro. A fruit preserve tastes different hot, when it has just been made, than it does when cooled. You will taste more sweet and sour flavors in warm, newly made preserves. These sensations overwhelm the aroma of the fruit and seasonings. Let your preserve cool and sit overnight before holding your critique. By that time the fruit essence and aroma will balance the flavors in the mouth. Fruit preserves are rarely eaten straight out of the jar, so give some thought to pairing your preserves with bread and adding them to desserts as ingredients or toppings.

WHAT TO DO WHEN THE JELLY WON'T JELL

From time to time, the desired jell does not occur as predicted, even when you think you've done everything correctly. You then have two choices. First, you can change your expectations and decide that what you really wanted was a sauce for ice cream or pancakes. There are recipes in the dessert chapter to help you with this modification.

Second, if you'd like to try to save your preserves, you can use this formula to jell them if they are thickened but syrupy:

- Measure and return the jelly to a boil.
- Melt ¼ cup Apple Jelly (see page 92) for every cup of jelly.
- Add melted Apple Jelly by the tablespoon along with a teaspoon of lemon juice until the jell point is reached and the jelly passes the cold plate test.
- Pour the preserves out again into a clean glass measure and follow directions for filling and vacuum-sealing jars.

JAR LIFTER

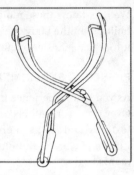

This sturdy tool looks like a medieval torture device, but it actually protects the preserver from possible splashes of scalding water. No other device will lift jars as safely into a hot water bath from a cooling rack and back again. The jar lifter is available in hardware stores wherever canning supplies are sold.

FRESH VS. FROZEN FRUIT

The recipes in this book are designed for fresh fruits and berries. Dry-packed frozen fruits can be substituted in a pinch with this cautionary advice:

- Move fruits to the refrigerator to thaw completely before cooking them. Frozen fruits exude more juice when defrosted. They may need less time to concentrate the juices.
- The flavor of frozen fruit is not as vibrant as fresh. To minimize this deficit, add a teaspoon more lemon juice per cup to accentuate the fruit flavor. You can also heighten the fruit's flavor by further reducing its juices. Or you can go in another direction and combine the frozen fruit with a complementary fresh fruit.

DOUBLING AND TRIPLING RECIPES

Yes, these recipes can be doubled or tripled, but it's not advisable for the best results. After spending a day picking peaches or berries, you may feel pressured to process your bounty quickly. Remember, fresh produce will keep well for a day or two in the refrigerator, giving you time to work in small batches.

CHAPTER

3

Jams

A FRUIT JAM IS EASY FOR beginning preservers to master. Fruit is simply cooked and sweetened, to taste. Recipes recommend the amount of sugar and lemon juice to add. This gives you time to inhale the rich scent of simmering fruit and to plan how you will serve it. Your success is guaranteed.

Despite its simplicity, my directions ask you to prepare these preserves with care. Attention to detail guarantees better results. You'll be asked, for example, to cut pineapple into wedges in one recipe and pulverize it in another. Pears are diced in one recipe and thinly sliced in another. As each pound of fruit or berries cooks and reduces (to about 1 cup of pulp and concentrated juices), these initial shapes will affect the jam's texture. This will become the jam's mouthfeel. As you gain experience in making preserves, you will learn to recognize the characteristic crunch of slender apple slices and the slippery feel of pineapple strands on the tongue as physical sensations essential to the taste of jam. Anticipating these nuances adds to the pleasure of preserving at home.

Another way to affect the consistency of jam is by limiting or extending the cooking time, depending on whether you prefer a looser or thicker jam. The amount of sugar added to the pan is also variable. The sweeter fruit ingredients may call for as little as ½ cup of sugar per cup of reduced fruit.

Blueberries, for example, need minimal sweetening and cooking to offer their characteristic fragrance and soft texture. A tart fruit, such as rhubarb, in contrast, will require a cup or more of sugar to sweeten the same volume. I have tried to minimize the amount of sugar so that the fruit flavor dominates. You can vary this to suit your taste without compromising the recipe.

You may be surprised to find that jams made with high-pectin fruits such as blueberry, blackberry, cranberry, and black raspberry will jell without your intending them to do so. Leaving them in this chapter is a signal that high pectin fruits jell easily.

Technique for Making Jams

- Prepare the fruit for preserving.
- Measure the sugar, and reserve it.
- Begin cooking with the pot covered and the heat at medium. Once simmering, uncover and simmer as directed.
- Add lemon juice and sugar as directed.
- Cook for a specified time, until a temperature is reached, or until a desired thickness of texture is achieved.
- Vacuum seal the preserves as directed.

Strawberry Jam

Chamomile tea adds the scent of newly mown hay to the bright sweetness of strawberries. It's an exhilarating treat to prepare in early spring.

- **2** pounds strawberries (8 cups quartered)
- **½** cup water
- **2** tablespoons lemon juice
- **1** cup sugar
- **2** bags chamomile tea (optional)

Rinse, stem, and quarter the strawberries. Combine them with the water in a nonreactive 5-quart saucepan. Cover and bring to a boil. Uncover and simmer for 10 minutes, stirring occasionally to prevent sticking.

Stir in the lemon juice, and add the sugar ½ cup at a time, waiting for the liquid to return to the boil before adding more. Continue simmering another 5 minutes, stirring frequently. Cook only until the jam threatens to stick to the pot.

Pour the jam into a 1-quart measure. Submerge 2 bags of chamomile tea, if desired. Press the bags against the side of the container and steep for 10 minutes. Remove the bags.

Fill the hot, sterilized jars to within ¼ inch of the lip. Wipe each rim clean, attach a new lid, and screw the cap on tightly. Proceed as directed to vacuum seal the jars in a water bath as described on page 20.

Strawberry Rhubarb Jam

YIELD
5½ CUPS

Although this classic combination is delicious on Risen Biscuits (see page 182) and English Muffins (see page 186), you can turn it into the main event in a number of desserts. Fill a pre-baked tart shell with jam, and decorate it with fresh strawberry halves and a red currant glaze. If the weather is too hot for baking, freeze it, diluted with a simple syrup or light cream for a spectacular soft-frozen treat. The sensuous blend of silken rhubarb strands and soft berries is delicious at any temperature.

2 pounds strawberries

1 pound rhubarb

1 cup water

10 strips lemon peel (approximately 3 inches long and ¼ inch wide)

Juice of 1 lemon

2 cups sugar

Rinse and drain the berries. Remove the stems, cut berries into a uniform size, and place them in a heavy, non-reactive 8-quart pan. Rinse, trim, and cut rhubarb into ½-inch lengths and add to the berries. Add the lemon peel strips and water. Cover the pot and bring liquid to a boil. Simmer, uncovered, for 15 minutes.

Add lemon juice, then the sugar ½ cup at a time, waiting until liquids come to a simmer again before adding more. Continue to cook on medium heat for 10 minutes, stirring regularly to keep the mixture from sticking to the bottom of the pan. Jam will reach a temperature of 212°F. When the bubbles are thick and the jam spits when stirred, take the pan off the heat.

Skim off the foam. Fill the hot, sterilized jars to within ¼ inch of the lip. Wipe each rim clean, attach a new lid, and screw the cap on tightly. Proceed as directed to vacuum seal the jars in a water bath as described on page 20.

Rhubarb Fig Jam

Bits of dried figs remain intact in this jam and leave nuggets of pure sweetness scattered throughout the tangy rhubarb strands. This bold texture is the key to the exciting play of sweet, sour, and astringent sensations on the palate.

Prolong this eating pleasure by spreading this jam on English Muffins (see page 186), or tone it down with a muffin of contrasting texture such as Grape-Nuts Muffins (see page 166) or Banana Bran Muffins (see page 167).

- **2** pounds rhubarb stalks
- **12** ounces dried Calamata figs
- **1** cup water
- **1** tablespoon fresh lemon juice
- **1½** cups sugar

Rinse, trim, and cut rhubarb into ½-inch pieces. Cut off tough tips of fig stems, and cut each fig into 8 bits. Place the figs on the bottom of a deep, non-reactive 5-quart pan, followed by the rhubarb. Pour in the water, cover, and bring liquid to a boil. Uncover and simmer for 10 minutes, stirring occasionally to prevent sticking.

Add lemon juice and then the sugar ½ cup at a time. Return to a boil for 10 minutes or until the jam is thick and holds its shape when cooled on a chilled plate.

Fill the hot, sterilized jars to within ¼ inch of the lip. Wipe each rim clean, attach a new lid, and screw the cap on tightly. Proceed as directed to vacuum seal the jars in a water bath as described on page 20.

Apple Ginger Jam

Not to be confused with applesauce, this soft preserve contains firm apple bits and chewy fragments of peel. The addition of tart lemon juice and tingling gingerroot seasoning guarantees a good balance of sweet, sour, and spicy sensations.

This jam would taste great on Apple Cinnamon Muffins (see page 164) or Buttermilk Currant Scones (see page 173). You could easily use it to make an Apple Jam Tart garnished with fresh apple slices (see page 204), or freeze it using the Philadelphia-Style Ice Cream recipe (see page 195). Wouldn't creamy apple ginger ice cream served with a warm burnt caramel sauce make a wonderful dessert?

- **1** cup water
- **½** tablespoon fresh lemon juice
- **2** pounds apples (use half Granny Smith, half Macintosh)
- **3** slices fresh ginger (size of a quarter)
- **2½** cups sugar
- Zest of 1 lemon

Combine water and lemon juice in a heavy, non-reactive 5-quart pot. Scrub and rinse the apples. Quarter, core, and dice the apples, leaving the skin attached. (Dice apple quarters, in two batches, in the food processor, using a pulsing action.) Immediately toss apple pieces into the acidulated water. Add the ginger slices, cover, and bring to a boil. Uncover and simmer for 10 to 15 minutes until most liquid is reduced.

Begin adding the sugar ½ cup at a time, allowing the liquid to regain the boil before adding more. Stir in thin strips of lemon peel removed with a zester. Lower the heat as the jam thickens, and cook another 5 minutes.

Off the heat, remove the ginger slices. Fill the hot, sterilized jars to within ¼ inch of the lip. Wipe each rim clean, attach a new lid, and screw the cap on tightly. Proceed as directed to vacuum seal the jars in a water bath as described on page 20.

Ginger Pear Jam

YIELD
3 CUPS

A fresh, knobby piece of gingerroot is an indispensable compliment to many fruit preserves. This spice generates a surge of warmth on the tongue and a spicy fragrance that enhances the delicate floral aroma and taste of pears. Here, as elsewhere, the lemon juice adds just enough acid to balance and flavor the other ingredients. Savor the pleasures of this taste-tingling jam on Risen Biscuits (see page 182) or warm Cream Scones (see page 172).

3 pounds Bartlett pears

½ cup water

1 tablespoon fresh lemon juice

2 slices fresh gingerroot (size of a quarter)

1 cup sugar

Peel, quarter, and core the pears. Coarsely chop them. Combine pears in a heavy, non-reactive 5-quart pan with water, lemon juice, and ginger slices. Cover and bring mixture to a boil. Uncover and simmer for 15 minutes, stirring occasionally.

Add sugar ½ cup at a time, allowing the liquid to regain the boil before adding more. Continue cooking, uncovered, for another 10 minutes, stirring more frequently, until the jam is thickened.

Remove the ginger slices and fill the hot, sterilized jars to within ¼ inch of the lip. Wipe each rim clean, attach a new lid, and screw the cap on tightly. Proceed as directed to vacuum seal the jars in a water bath as described on page 20.

Pear and Pineapple Jam

YIELD
3½ CUPS

Pears and pineapples, so different in taste and texture, make a wonderfully harmonious preserve that respects the consistency, flavor, and scent of both. A plateful of Oatmeal Muffins (see page 163) or Drop Scones (see page 174) would complement this jam well.

2 pounds Bartlett pears

1 pound peeled and cored pineapple

½ cup water

1 tablespoon fresh lemon juice

1 cup sugar

 Zest from 1 lemon

Peel, quarter, and core pears. Cut pears and pineapple into pieces the size of lima beans. (If you are using a food processor, cut each fruit separately with the steel blade, making rapid on-and-off motions.)

Combine fruits with water and lemon juice in a heavy, non-reactive 5-quart pan. Cover and bring to a boil. Uncover and simmer for 15 minutes, stirring occasionally.

Add sugar ½ cup at a time, allowing the liquid to regain the boil before adding more. Continue cooking for 10 minutes, stirring frequently to prevent sticking. An instant-reading thermometer will rise to 212–214°F as the jam reduces to 3½ cups. Off the heat, stir in the lemon zest removed with a zester (illustrated on page 16).

Fill the hot, sterilized jars to within ¼ inch of the lip. Wipe each rim clean, attach a new lid, and screw the cap on tightly. Proceed as directed to vacuum seal the jars in a water bath as described on page 20.

Pear and Plum Jam

YIELD
4½ CUPS

Although they rarely appear together, pears and plums are quite compatible fruits. This recipe offers a quick and easy way to preserve their summer-fresh flavors and aromas for cold-weather breakfasts or tea served with English Muffins (see page 186) or Grape-Nuts Muffins (see page 166).

2	pounds Bartlett pears
1½	pounds Italian plums
⅓	cup water
1	tablespoon fresh lemon juice
1	cup sugar

Peel, quarter, and core the pears. Scrub and rinse the plums. Halve plums and remove their pits. Chop fruits into ½-inch pieces. (If you are using a food processor, process each fruit separately with pulsing action.) Combine the fruit pieces with water in a heavy, non-reactive 5-quart pan. Cover and bring to a boil. Uncover and simmer for 10 minutes, stirring occasionally.

Add lemon juice and sugar ½ cup at a time, allowing the liquid to regain the boil before adding more. Continue cooking, stirring frequently, until there is little standing liquid on top of the fruit pulp. Remove from the heat when bubbles begin to heave with a noisy plopping sound.

Fill the hot, sterilized jars to within ¼ inch of the lip. Wipe each rim clean, attach a new lid, and screw the cap on tightly. Proceed as directed to vacuum seal the jars in a water bath as described on page 20.

Raspberry Pear Jam

YIELD
4 CUPS

Red raspberries and pears make a dynamic pair that taste wonderful served fresh or cooked, hot or cold. This jam is delicious spread on a warm English Muffin (see page 186) or Cream Scone (see page 172).

1 pound Bartlett pears

1½ pounds red raspberries

⅓ cup water

2 tablespoons lemon juice

2 cups sugar

Peel, quarter, core, and dice the pears. Combine them with raspberries and water in a heavy, non-reactive 5-quart saucepan. Cover and bring to a boil. Uncover and simmer for 10 minutes.

Add lemon juice and sugar ½ cup at a time, allowing the liquid to regain the boil before adding more. Partly cover the pot to prevent spattering when necessary. Also stir frequently to prevent sticking. Total cooking time will be about 15 minutes or until a finished temperature reading of 212°F is attained. Jam will reduce to 1 quart.

Fill the hot, sterilized jars to within ¼ inch of the lip. Wipe each rim clean, attach a new lid, and screw the cap on tightly. Proceed as directed to vacuum seal the jars in a water bath as described on page 20.

Cherry Red Raspberry Jam

YIELD
4½ CUPS

The red raspberries in this jam accentuate the less assertive flavor of the cherries. I serve this jam on special occasions and give it as gifts to friends. It is terrific on Butter Pecan Muffins (see page 162), Cream Scones (see page 172), and English Muffins (see page 186).

- **2** pounds pitted sour cherries (4 cups)
- **1** pound red raspberries (1½ pints)
- **2** tablespoons fresh lemon juice
- **2½** cups sugar

Place the cherries in the bowl of a food processor or blender and pulse for 15 seconds to coarsely chop them. Combine cherries with raspberries in a heavy, non-reactive 8-quart pot, cover, and bring to a boil. Uncover and simmer for 15 minutes to reduce the juices, stirring regularly. The mixture will thicken but should not stick.

Stir in the lemon juice, and begin adding sugar ½ cup at a time, waiting for the liquid to return to the simmer before adding more. Continue to stir frequently. Let the jam cook 10 minutes more. It will thicken noticeably, and the temperature will reach 216–218°F.

Pour the jam into a heat-resistant glass quart measure. Stir twice over a 5-minute period.

Fill the hot, sterilized jars to within ¼ inch of the lip. Wipe each rim clean, attach a new lid, and screw the cap on tightly. Proceed as directed to vacuum seal the jars in a water bath as described on page 20.

Cherry Vanilla Jam

YIELD
4 CUPS

2 pounds pitted sour cherries (4 cups)

1 pound Granny Smith apples (2½ cups peeled and chopped)

1 vanilla bean or 1 tablespoon vanilla paste or extract

2 tablespoons fresh lemon juice

2¼ cups sugar

Place the cherries in the bowl of a food processor or blender and pulse for 15 seconds to chop them medium-fine. Peel, core, and quarter the apples. Chop them to a medium-fine texture in the food processor or blender, using a pulsing action. Combine the cherry and apple pieces in a heavy, non-reactive 5-quart pan.

Cut through the skin of the vanilla pod along its length. Use a paring knife to scrape the contents of the pod onto the knife. Add the vanilla pod and scraped beans to the fruit. Cover the pan and bring to a boil. Uncover and simmer for 15 minutes to reduce the juices, stirring regularly. The mixture will thicken but should not stick.

Stir in the lemon juice, then add sugar in four equal batches, waiting for the liquid to return to the simmer before adding more. Continue to stir frequently. Let the jam cook actively 10 minutes more. It will noticeably thicken and reach a temperature of 210–212°F.

Pour the jam into a heat-resistant 1-quart measure. Remove the vanilla pod or add the vanilla paste. Fill the hot, sterilized jars to within ¼ inch of the lip. Wipe each rim clean, attach a new lid, and screw the cap on tightly. Proceed as directed to vacuum seal the jars in a water bath as described on page 20.

Red and Black Raspberry Jam with Cherries

YIELD
5 CUPS

- **1** pound black raspberries (1½ pints)
- **1** pound red raspberries (1½ pints)
- **1** pound pitted sour cherries (2 cups)
- **½** cup water
- **2** tablespoons lemon juice
- **2¾** cups sugar

Combine cherries with raspberries and water in a heavy, non-reactive 5-quart pan, cover, and bring to a boil. Uncover and simmer for 15 minutes to reduce the juices, stirring regularly. The mixture will thicken but should not stick.

Add the lemon juice, then begin adding sugar ½ cup at a time, waiting for the liquid to return to the simmer before adding more. Continue to stir frequently. Let the jam cook 10 minutes more. It will noticeably thicken and the candy thermometer will read 216°F.

Fill the hot, sterilized jars to within ¼ inch of the lip. Wipe each rim clean, attach a new lid, and screw the cap on tightly. Proceed as directed to vacuum seal the jars in a water bath as described on page 20.

Black Raspberry Cassis Jam

YIELD
3 CUPS

2 pints black raspberries

2 pints black currants

½ cup water

2 tablespoons lemon juice

3 cups sugar

Rinse and combine the raspberries and currants. Place fruit in a non-reactive 5-quart saucepan. Pour in water, cover the pan, and bring to a boil. Uncover and simmer 15 minutes.

Remove seeds and skins by passing berries through the finest disk of a food mill. If the combined pulp and juice is less than 3 cups, add water to measure that amount. If the purée is more than 3 cups, increase amount of sugar called for to equal the same volume as the fruit.

Return mixture and lemon juice to a clean pan, and bring to a simmer, stirring frequently to prevent the pulp from sticking to the bottom. Add the sugar ½ cup at a time, waiting for the jam to return to a boil before adding more. Stir the pot after each addition to prevent the pulp from sticking.

Cook the jam at medium-high heat, stirring frequently, for 5 minutes longer. The thermometer will reach 216–218°F, and the jam will be very thick. This jam will coat the spoon generously.

Off the heat, transfer the preserves to a 1-quart measure. Fill the hot, sterilized jars to within ¼ inch of the lip. Wipe each rim clean, attach a new lid, and screw the cap on tightly. Proceed as directed to vacuum seal the jars in a water bath as described on page 20.

Seedless Black Raspberry Jam

YIELD

3 CUPS

The concentrated essence of wild black raspberries in this jam recalls the cool, damp air trapped in wooded raspberry thickets on hot afternoons in early July.

- **4** pints black raspberries (2½ pounds)
- **½** cup water
- **2** tablespoons fresh lemon juice
- **3½** cups sugar

Rinse berries and combine with water in a heavy, non-reactive 5-quart pan. Cover and bring to a simmer. Simmer, partially covered, for 10 minutes. Use a food mill fitted with the disk with the smallest openings to separate the juices and pulp from the seeds. The result will measure 3½ cups. If there is less, add water to measure that amount. If there is more, increase sugar called for to equal the same volume as the fruit pulp.

Pour the black raspberry pulp and the lemon juice into a clean 5-quart pan. Return to the simmer, and begin adding sugar ½ cup at a time, allowing the juices to return to a boil before adding more. Stir the pan each time you add sugar to prevent the pulp from sticking to the bottom. Cook over medium-high heat, now stirring every minute, until jam reaches 216–218°F. This should happen in 5 to 7 minutes. The preserves will be quite thick.

Fill the hot, sterilized jars to within ¼ inch of the lip. Wipe each rim clean, attach a new lid, and screw the cap on tightly. Proceed as directed to vacuum seal the jars in a water bath as described on page 20.

Rhubarb Ginger Jam

YIELD
3 CUPS

Rhubarb jam with ginger was one of the first fruit preserves I ever made. I was thrilled with its dramatic balance of tart rhubarb, hot ginger, and sweet sugar.

I recommend you first try this jam on chewy English Muffins (see page 186) so you can fully enjoy the taste and texture of clusters of rhubarb strands and exciting hot tiny bits of crystallized ginger.

- **2** pounds fresh rhubarb
- **8** 3-inch strips lemon peel (approximately ¼ inch wide)
- **2** fresh gingerroot slices (size of a quarter)
- **½** cup water
- **1** tablespoon lemon juice
- **2½** cups sugar
- **2** ounces (⅓ cup) thinly sliced crystallized ginger

Rinse, trim, and cut fresh rhubarb stalks into ½-inch lengths. Combine with lemon strips (removed with a stripper, illustrated on page 16), gingerroot slices, and water in a heavy, non-reactive 5-quart pan. Cover and bring to a boil. Uncover and simmer for 10 minutes, stirring occasionally.

Add lemon juice and sugar ½ cup at a time, waiting for the liquid to return to the boil before adding more. Continue cooking over high heat, stirring constantly, until the jam thickens and bubble pattern becomes quite dense. Stir in the crystallized ginger pieces at the end of the cooking period.

Off the heat, remove the gingerroot. Fill the hot, sterilized jars to within ¼ inch of the lip. Wipe each rim clean, attach a new lid, and screw the cap on tightly. Proceed as directed to vacuum seal the jars in a water bath as described on page 20.

Rhubarb Blackberry Jam

YIELD
3 CUPS

Since fresh rhubarb and blackberries are not always available at the market at the same time, you will have to supply your own from the garden or substitute a frozen product for one of the fruits. Let the frozen fruit come almost to room temperature before starting the recipe. The frozen fruit will exude more liquid than the fresh and may require a slightly longer cooking time. Serve this jam with any one of the chewy English Muffin recipes (see page 186).

¾	pound rhubarb
1	pound fresh blackberries
½	cup water
1	tablespoon lemon juice
1¾	cups sugar

Rinse and trim rhubarb. Cut it into ½-inch lengths. Combine rhubarb and blackberries with water in a heavy, non-reactive 5-quart pan. Cover and bring to a boil. Uncover and simmer for 10 minutes until the fruits soften and release juice but remain whole.

Add lemon juice, then sugar in three equal batches, returning the liquid to the boil after each addition. Stir jam continuously until it thickens noticeably and the bubble pattern is quite dense. Temperature of jam should be 210°F.

Fill the hot, sterilized jars to within ¼ inch of the lip. Wipe each rim clean, attach a new lid, and screw the cap on tightly. Proceed as directed to vacuum seal the jars in a water bath as described on page 20.

Apricot Blueberry Jam

The cooking time for this jam is short, and little sugar is added, so the generous yield of soft, reduced fruit pieces is intensely fresh tasting. This jam is delicious served with Zucchini Bread (see page 169) or Grape-Nuts Muffins (see page 166).

2 pounds apricots (4 cups after peeling and pitting)

½ cup water

1 pound blueberries

2 tablespoons lemon juice

1 cup sugar

Dip the apricots in boiling water for 30 seconds. Move them to an iced water bath. When cool enough to handle, slip off their skins, remove pits, and slice apricots. Combine apricots with water in a heavy, non-reactive 5-quart saucepan. Cover and bring to a boil. Uncover and simmer, stirring frequently, for 5 minutes.

Rinse the blueberries and stir them into the apricot mixture. Cover and bring the jam back to the simmer. Uncover and cook for 10 minutes.

Add lemon juice, then sugar ½ cup at a time, waiting for the liquid to return to the boil before adding more. Continue cooking over high heat, stirring constantly, until the jam thickens and the bubble pattern becomes quite dense. The jam should pass the cold plate test.

Fill the hot, sterilized jars to within ¼ inch of the lip. Wipe each rim clean, attach a new lid, and screw the cap on tightly. Proceed as directed to vacuum seal the jars in a water bath as described on page 20.

Apricot Orange Jam

YIELD

3 CUPS

The acidic bite of orange juice and its fresh citrus scent accentuate the perfumed sweetness of the apricots. Together they make a sunny, light preserve that is perfect for a brunch buffet, spread on freshly baked Risen Biscuits (see page 182) or Cornmeal Muffins (see page 160).

2 pounds ripe apricots

1 6-ounce can unsweetened orange juice concentrate

¾ cup water

1¼ cups sugar

Zest of 1 orange

¼ cup apricot liqueur

Dip the apricots in boiling water for 30 seconds. Move them to an iced water bath. When cool enough to handle, slip off their skins, remove pits, and slice apricots. Combine the slices with orange juice concentrate and water in a heavy, non-reactive 5-quart pan. Cover and bring to a boil. Uncover and simmer for 10 minutes, stirring regularly. Apricot slices will cook and soften. As the mixture thickens, bubbles will become small and tightly packed. Portions of it will begin to heave and plop.

Add the sugar in three equal batches, waiting for the liquid to return to a boil before adding more. Continue to stir and simmer on low for 10 minutes. Add orange zest and liqueur, and cook another 2 minutes to thicken jam a bit more. Stir continuously at this point to prevent sticking.

Fill the hot, sterilized jars to within ¼ inch of the lip. Wipe each rim clean, attach a new lid, and screw the cap on tightly. Proceed as directed to vacuum seal the jars in a water bath as described on page 20.

Peach Blueberry Jam

YIELD
3½ CUPS

A jam made with sliced peaches and blueberries retains fresh and delicate fruit flavors when it is cooked briefly and gently. Enjoy the subtlety of this jam with Cream Scones (see page 172), Risen Biscuits (see page 182), or Oatmeal Muffins (see page 163).

- **2** pounds peaches (3 cups)
- **½** cup water
- **1** pound blueberries
- **2** tablespoons lemon juice
- **3** cups sugar

Dip the peaches in boiling water for 30 seconds. Move to an iced water bath. When cool enough to handle, peel off the skins, pit, and thinly slice. Combine peach slices with the water in a deep, non-reactive 5-quart saucepan. Cover and bring to a boil. Uncover and simmer, stirring frequently, for 10 minutes. Peaches will become thick with bubbles. The pot will make a hissing sound as you pull the spoon across the bottom, but the peach pulp will not stick.

Stir in the blueberries, cover the pan, and return the mixture to a boil. Uncover and simmer for 10 minutes. Add lemon juice, then sugar ½ cup at a time, waiting for the liquid to return to a boil before adding more. Simmer for 5 minutes or until thickened. A thermometer reading at this point should be 210°F.

Fill the hot, sterilized jars to within ¼ inch of the lip. Wipe each rim clean, attach a new lid, and screw the cap on tightly. Proceed as directed to vacuum seal the jars in a water bath as described on page 20.

Kiwifruit Pineapple Jam

YIELD
3½ CUPS

Kiwifruit is a newcomer to preserving. Originally a native of New Zealand, kiwifruit is now grown in California and available throughout the year at reasonable prices. Its acid-green color and tiny black seeds are quite dramatic but fade as you cook it.

The pineapple and kiwifruit have similar flavor profiles. They are lusciously sweet when ripe but acidic to the point of astringency before that. The sugar you add will temper the fruit acid and allow their distinct and complementary tastes to mingle.

6 large kiwifruits (3 cups)

1½ pounds peeled and cored pineapple (4 cups)

½ cup water

2 tablespoons lemon juice

3 cups sugar

Peel and quarter kiwifruits lengthwise. Slice quarters into thin pie-shaped wedges. (If using a food processor, chop 3 kiwifruits at a time, quartered, with rapid on and off motions, until they are ½-inch bits.)

Chop the pineapple into ¼-inch wedges, or chop with rapid pulsing in the food processor.

Combine the pineapple, kiwifruit pieces, and water in a heavy, non-reactive 5-quart pan. Cover and bring to a boil. Uncover and simmer for 10 minutes.

Add lemon juice, then sugar ½ cup at a time, waiting for the liquid to return to a boil before adding more. Continue to boil for 10 more minutes or until the jam reaches 216°F.

Off the heat, skim foam from the surface. Fill the hot, sterilized jars to within ¼ inch of the lip. Wipe each rim clean, attach a new lid, and screw the cap on tightly. Proceed as directed to vacuum seal the jars in a water bath as described on page 20.

Kiwifruit Mint Jam

YIELD

2⅔ CUPS

A touch of citrus fragrance and the cool, soothing sensation of fresh mint in this kiwifruit jam highlight the considerable flavor range of this fuzzy little fruit. It is sweet, a bit acidic (particularly before it ripens), and its scent recalls ripe bananas and strawberries. Savor the subtlety of this jam spread on English Muffins (see page 186) or a Cream Scone (see page 172).

- **2** pounds ripe kiwifruit
- **⅓** cup water
- **2** tablespoons lemon juice
- **2** cups sugar
- Zest of 1 lemon
- **3** 6-inch sprigs fresh mint

Peel and quarter kiwifruit. Slice thinly and combine with water in a heavy, non-reactive 5-quart pan. Cover and bring to a boil. Uncover and simmer for 10 minutes, stirring every 2 to 3 minutes.

Add lemon juice, then sugar ½ cup at a time, waiting for the liquid to return to a boil before adding more. Continue cooking briskly and stirring until jam mixture thickens and there is a tight pattern of bubbles over the top. This will happen in less than 5 minutes. The temperature of the hot liquid should be 212°F.

Off the heat, pour the jam into a 1-quart measure. Stir in the lemon zest and mint sprigs. Crush the mint stems along the bottom and sides of the container. Let mint steep in the jam for 5 minutes. Cool a spoonful of jam and taste. Remove the stems when the scent of mint is mild and complementary.

Fill the hot, sterilized jars to within ¼ inch of the lip. Wipe each rim clean, attach a new lid, and screw the cap on tightly. Proceed as directed to vacuum seal the jars in a water bath as described on page 20.

Nectarine Jam with Grand Marnier

YIELD

3½ CUPS

The nectarine is a fuzzless peach, both sweeter and more acidic. Serve this mellow jam with Grape-Nuts Muffins (see page 166) or Butter Pecan Muffins (see page 162).

3 pounds ripe nectarines (5½ cups)

⅓ cup water

1 cup sugar

¼ cup Grand Marnier liqueur

2 tablespoons fresh lemon juice

Submerge the nectarines for 30 seconds in boiling water. Cool them immediately in a bowl of iced water. Peel them when cool enough to handle. Cut the meat away from the stone and chop into small pieces. You will have about 5½ cups of fruit.

Combine nectarine pieces with water in a heavy, non-reactive 5-quart saucepan. Cover and bring to a boil. Uncover and simmer for 10 minutes, stirring occasionally to prevent sticking.

Stir in the sugar ½ cup at a time, returning liquid to a simmer before adding more. Allow liquid to reduce over medium heat, stirring frequently. This will take about 15 minutes. When the jam thickens noticeably, stir, and pour in the Grand Marnier and lemon juice. Reduce quickly, stirring constantly for another 2 minutes.

Fill hot, sterilized jars to within ¼ inch of the lip. Wipe the rims clean, attach new lids, and screw caps on tightly. Proceed as directed to vacuum seal the jars in a water bath as described on page 20.

Pineapple Blueberry Jam

A jam of pineapple and blueberries is bound to contain rich contrasts in taste, texture, and scent. A fresh, warm plateful of English Muffins (see page 186) and cold sweet butter are definitely in order for sampling it.

- **1¼** pounds peeled and cored pineapple
- **⅓** cup water
- **1½** tablespoons fresh lime juice
- **1½** cups sugar, divided
- **1** pound fresh blueberries

Chop the pineapple into ¼-inch wedges, or chop with rapid pulsing in the food processor. Combine pineapple pieces and water in a heavy, non-reactive 5-quart saucepan. Cover and bring to a boil. Uncover and simmer for 15 minutes or until almost all juice is reduced.

Stir in the lime juice, then add ½ cup sugar. Boil, uncovered, for 10 minutes, stirring frequently. Stop cooking if fruit pieces threaten to stick to the bottom.

Stir in the blueberries, cover the pan, and return jam to a simmer. Uncover and cook 10 minutes, stirring regularly. Add the remaining cup of sugar, ½ cup at a time. Cook the jam over medium-high heat for another 5 minutes, stirring every minute or so. Jam is ready when liquid passes the spoon test (page 16). A thermometer should register 210°F.

Fill hot, sterilized jars to within ¼ inch of the lip. Wipe rims clean, attach new lids, and screw caps on tightly. Proceed as directed to vacuum seal the jars in a water bath as described on page 20.

Spicy Tomato Prune Jam

YIELD
4 CUPS

This recipe is for the more adventuresome cook who seeks out new taste experiences. Tomatoes and prunes make quite a mild, sweet blend; the red wine vinegar added at the very end adds contrast and accentuates the ingredients. This soft, spreadable jam is great on warm Oatmeal Muffins (see page 163) and Buttermilk Currant Scones (see page 173).

12 ounces pitted prunes

2 pounds ripe tomatoes (4–5 medium)

Bouquet garni: 1 cinnamon stick, 3 cloves, 3 allspice berries, 2 lemon peel strips

2 tablespoons lemon juice

½ cup granulated sugar

½ cup brown sugar

1 tablespoon (or more to taste) red wine vinegar

Cut prunes into ½-inch pieces. Dip the tomatoes in simmering water for 30 seconds. Cool in an iced water bath. When cool enough to handle, slip off the skins, then core and quarter the tomatoes. Force out seeds into a fine strainer and reserve the juices. Coarsely chop tomato pieces.

Combine prunes, tomatoes, strained juices, and bouquet garni seasoning wrapped in cloth in a deep, non-reactive 4-quart saucepan. Cover and bring to a simmer. Uncover and simmer for 15 minutes, stirring regularly. (The mixture will thicken and be free of standing liquid.)

Stir in the lemon juice, then the sugars one at a time. Continue cooking for another 10 minutes until the jam is thick again and a thermometer reads 208–210°F.

Off the heat, remove the bouquet and stir in the vinegar. Quickly cool a tablespoon of jam in the freezer and taste for the slightly tart finish of the vinegar to balance the sweet fruits. Add more vinegar if desired.

Fill hot, sterilized jars to within ¼ inch of the lip. Wipe the rims clean, attach new lids, and screw caps on tightly. Vacuum seal in a water bath as described on page 20.

Tomato Basil Jam

YIELD

2½–3 CUPS

Balance is important here. You will want to cool and taste this jam carefully to bring sweet and sour elements into equilibrium. Add the remaining basil strips as the jam cools so they retain their vivid green color.

3 pounds ripe tomatoes

2 lemons

24 fresh basil leaves, divided

1 cup sugar

Dip the tomatoes in simmering water for 30 seconds. Cool them in an iced water bath. When cool enough to handle, peel, core, quarter, and squeeze seeds out though a sieve to retain juices. Coarsely chop the tomatoes. Pieces and reserved juice will measure a generous 4 cups.

Place tomatoes in a deep, non-reactive 4-quart pan. Cover and bring to a boil. Uncover and simmer for 30 minutes or until the jam is reduced to 2½ to 3 cups and free of excess moisture.

While the tomatoes simmer, remove the yellow zest from the 2 lemons with a zester (illustrated on page 16). Squeeze the juice from both lemons. Purée 12 basil leaves with ½ of the lemon juice.

Off the heat, stir the zest and the lemon juice without the basil into the tomatoes. Return the tomato mixture to a simmer, and begin adding the sugar ½ cup at a time, allowing the mixture to regain the boil before adding more. Cook and stir frequently for 10 minutes, until the jam thickens again. The thermometer reading should be 210°F.

Off the heat, stir in remaining lemon-basil juice. Cool a tablespoon of jam briefly. When cooled to room temperature, taste for a balance of sweet and sour. Add more lemon juice by the tablespoon as needed. Cut the remaining basil leaves into thin strips. Fold them into the jam.

Fill hot, sterilized jars to within ¼ inch of the lip. Wipe rims clean, attach new lids, and screw caps on tightly. Vacuum seal in a water bath as described on page 20.

Spicy Tomato Orange Jam

This jam celebrates my favorite winter lunch drink, a mug of hot V-8 juice flavored with a little orange juice and scented with spices. You can warm the jam if you like by heating it in the oven. Try it on fresh Cornmeal Muffins (see page 160).

3 pounds ripe tomatoes

2 navel oranges

Bouquet garni: 3 cloves, 3 allspice berries, 1 slice fresh gingerroot

1 cup sugar

2 tablespoons unsweetened orange juice concentrate (optional)

Tomato paste (optional)

Submerge tomatoes in boiling water for 30 seconds. Move to an iced water bath. When cool enough to handle, peel, core, and quarter. Force out seeds and liquid through a sieve; coarsely chop the pulp. Tomato pieces and strained juices will measure about 4 cups.

Remove the zest from both oranges with a zester (illustrated on page 16). Cut away and discard inner white peel. Halve the oranges, remove seeds, and thinly slice.

Combine tomatoes and juices with orange zest, orange slices, and the bouquet garni spices wrapped in cloth in a deep, non-reactive 4-quart saucepan. Cover and bring to a boil. Uncover and simmer for 25 minutes or until the mixture has reduced to 3 cups.

Stir in sugar ½ cup at a time, allowing the jam to return to the simmer between additions. Cook at a simmer for another 10 minutes until reduced again to about 3 cups. Temperature of mixture will reach 210°F.

Off the heat, remove bouquet garni. Cool a tablespoon of jam in the freezer and taste for an even blend of tomato and orange flavors. Add orange juice concentrate or a little tomato paste as needed for balance.

Fill the hot, sterilized jars to within ¼ inch of the lip. Wipe each rim clean, attach a new lid, and screw the cap on tightly. Proceed as directed to vacuum seal the jars in a water bath as described on page 20.

Green Tomato Jam

YIELD
2½ CUPS

You may be surprised to find that unripe tomatoes cook into a mild, sweet jam. The lemon, apple, and cinnamon add greater subtlety. Cornmeal Muffins (see page 160) and Buttermilk Currant Scones (see page 173) offer interesting taste and texture contrasts.

- **2** pounds green tomatoes
- **2** lemons
- **1** tart apple
- **½** cup water
- **1** 4-inch cinnamon stick
- **1** cup sugar

Scrub and rinse all of the fruits. Remove the stem ends of the tomatoes and dice them by hand or chop them two at a time, quartered, in a food processor fitted with a steel blade, using a rapid pulsing action. Remove the zest from the lemons with a zester (illustrated on page 16). Cut off and discard the inner white peel. Halve the lemons and thinly slice, removing seeds. Peel, quarter, core, and dice the apple.

Combine the tomatoes, lemon zest, lemon slices, and apple pieces with the water and cinnamon stick in a heavy, non-reactive 4-quart pan. Cover the pan and bring liquid to a boil. Uncover and simmer for 15 minutes.

Add sugar ½ cup at a time, allowing the jam to return to the simmer between additions. Cook, uncovered, for 10 minutes, stirring frequently. The temperature will rise to 210°F.

Off the heat, remove the cinnamon stick. Fill the hot, sterilized jars to within ¼ inch of the lip. Wipe each rim clean, attach a new lid, and screw the cap on tightly. Proceed as directed to vacuum seal the jars in a water bath as described on page 20.

Spicy Cranberry Jam

Why should the cranberry be relegated to salad molds and jelly in tins when it makes such an interesting preserve? This jam recipe is quite easy to prepare, and it makes a terrific topping for all holiday breads. Warm Butter Pecan Muffins (see page 162) or Whole-Wheat English Muffins (see page 187) are my bread choices from this book.

You could easily freeze this cranberry jam, using my sorbet formula (see page 194), and serve it as a festive and colorful palate freshener at the beginning or end of a rich winter meal.

2 pounds cranberries

½ cup water

Bouquet garni: 1 4-inch cinnamon stick, ½ teaspoon fennel seed, 2 whole cloves, 3 allspice berries, 1 slice gingerroot

4 cups sugar

Pick over and remove any bruised cranberries before weighing them. Rinse them and combine with water in a heavy, non-reactive 4-quart pan. Cover the pan and bring berries to a boil. Submerge bouquet garni wrapped in cloth in the cranberry mixture. Leave uncovered and simmer for 10 minutes.

Stir in the sugar, ½ cup at a time, allowing the jam to return to the boil before adding more. Partly cover the pot if jam begins to spit. Continue to cook until the jam thickens and the temperature rises to 214°F, but no more than 20 minutes.

Off the heat, let the spices steep an additional 5 minutes before removing them. Fill the hot, sterilized jars to within ¼ inch of the lip. Wipe each rim clean, attach a new lid, and screw the cap on tightly. Proceed as directed to vacuum seal the jars in a water bath as described on page 20.

Damson Plum Jam

YIELD
ABOUT 6 CUPS

Since these eggplant-purple plums ripen quickly and are not widely grown, you may have to look hard to find them at the market. They are intensely sour when fresh, but when cooked, their preserved essence of plum develops into a superb sweet-sour flavor.

This jam is crimson and spicy-sweet if cooked only to 214°F. As you continue to cook it to 218°F, it becomes darker, firmer, and more tart. Pair this assertive jam with vigorous breads such as Buckwheat Muffins (see page 165) or Tea Brack (see page 171).

4 pounds Damson plums

1 cup water

Sugar to equal the volume of cooked purée

Scrub, rinse, and stem plums. Combine plums and water in a heavy, non-reactive 8-quart pan. Cover and bring to a boil. Uncover and simmer for 30 minutes.

Let the cooked plums cool briefly, then pass them through a sieve or food mill to separate the pits and skins from the pulp. Measure the plum pulp, and set aside 1 cup sugar for every full cup of plum purée.

Place plum pulp in a clean 8-quart pan, cover, and heat slowly to a boil. Begin adding sugar about ½ cup at a time, allowing the jam to return to a boil between additions. After all the sugar is added, insert a thermometer and continue cooking, stirring frequently, until the temperature reaches 214°F.

Off the heat, give the jam the cold plate test (page 16). If you like the consistency, stop the cooking. For a firmer soft-jell jam, cook the jam another 5 minutes or to a temperature reading of up to 218°F. Stir almost constantly during this period.

Fill the hot, sterilized jars to within ¼ inch of the lip. Wipe each rim clean, attach a new lid, and screw the cap on tightly. Proceed as directed to vacuum seal the jars in a water bath as described on page 20.

Plum Jam with Cardamom

Plum skins have a pleasant acidic tang that invite the sweet fragrance of cardamom seeds. This assertive jam tastes best with an equally vigorous bread like Buckwheat Muffins (see page 165) or Whole-Wheat English Muffins (see page 187).

2 pounds Italian plums (3⅓ cups)

5 cardamom pods

⅓ cup water

1 cup sugar

Scrub and rinse the plums. Halve them, remove pits, and finely chop. (If you are using a food processor, cut the plums with a rapid pulsing action.) Tie cardamom pods in a piece of cloth with cotton twine and crush them lightly with a rolling pin. Combine them with the plums and water in a heavy, non-reactive 4-quart pan. Cover and bring to a boil. Uncover and simmer for 10 minutes.

Begin adding sugar ½ cup at a time, waiting for the mixture to regain the boil before adding more. Continue to cook, stirring regularly to prevent sticking, until the mixture is quite thick.

Off the heat, remove cardamom seeds. Fill the hot, sterilized jars to within ¼ inch of the lip. Wipe each rim clean, attach a new lid, and screw the cap on tightly. Vacuum seal in a water bath as described on page 20.

Quince Jam

YIELD
6 CUPS

A ripe quince gives off such a rich apple perfume that you may hesitate to cook yours, preferring instead to cluster a few in a bowl to place where their fragrance can be appreciated. Once you begin to prepare this fruit for cooking and see how hard and woody it is to cut, how positively astringent it is in the mouth, you will be convinced that the market sold you the wrong fruit. Don't give up. Cooking and sweetening it will thoroughly subdue and transform the quince into a soft and mild jam with a lovely apple scent. Enjoy the delicacy of Quince Jam on Oatmeal Muffins (see page 163) or Drop Scones (see page 174).

1 quart water

2 tablespoons fresh lemon juice, divided

3 pounds quinces

1½ cups sugar

Combine water with 1 tablespoon of lemon juice in a heavy, non-reactive 5-quart pan.

Peel, quarter, and core the quinces. Cut the quarters into eighths or smaller uniform pieces. As soon as each quince is cut, stir the pieces into the acidulated water. This will keep them from discoloring.

Cover the pan and bring liquid to a boil. Uncover and simmer for 30 minutes. Remove about half of the tender quince pieces from the pan. Cut these into small dice. Purée the remaining quince pieces with the liquid.

Return the quince pieces and the purée to a clean 5-quart saucepan. Cover and return to a boil. Uncover, add the remaining tablespoon of lemon juice, and begin adding the sugar ½ cup at a time, allowing the mixture to return to a boil before adding more. The jam will be quite thick and will require frequent stirring to prevent sticking. Cook until the jam will hold its shape on a spoon.

Fill the hot, sterilized jars to within ¼ inch of the lip. Wipe each rim clean, attach a new lid, and screw the cap on tightly. Proceed as directed to vacuum seal the jars in a water bath as described on page 20.

Blueberry Jam with Mint

YIELD
5 CUPS

This recipe is technically a hybrid, mixing two steps from the preserve technique with the jam process. The sugar is added cup for cup with the fruit, and it is cooked to the jell point. However, the berries are never strained, steeped, or reduced but remain whole in the pot during the entire cooking process, which is typical of jam making. The result is a larger than usual yield of a sweet, delicate jam that is lightly jelled.

Try this jam with Butter Pecan Muffins (see page 162), or pour it over hot French Toast (see page 180), Buckwheat Blinis (see page 178), or the Giant Sunday Popover (see page 175).

- **2** pounds fresh blueberries
- **½** cup water
- **2** tablespoons lemon juice
- **2** cups sugar
- **4** 6-inch sprigs fresh mint

Pick over the berries, rinse, and combine with water in a heavy, non-reactive 5-quart pan. Cover and bring mixture to a boil. Simmer, uncovered, for 10 minutes.

Add lemon juice, then begin adding sugar ½ cup at a time, allowing the mixture to regain the boil before adding more. Let jam boil for 5 minutes. It will be too thick to reach the jell point on a thermometer, but it will pass the plate test easily.

Pour the jam into a 2-quart measure. Submerge the mint sprigs tied with twine, crushing them against the sides and bottom of the container. Let them steep for 5 minutes, stirring occasionally. Remove the mint.

Fill the hot, sterilized jars to within ¼ inch of the lip. Wipe each rim clean, attach a new lid, and screw the cap on tightly. Proceed as directed to vacuum seal the jars in a water bath as described on page 20.

Boysenberry Jam

YIELD

3 CUPS

The Oregon boysenberries I used in this recipe were oblong and bristling with large, juicy lobes. They have an ambivalent taste, favoring neither parent from which they were bred, the raspberry or the blackberry. I took the initiative and added a little raspberry brandy.

If you enjoy the taste and texture of berry lobes, you will want to eat this jam on warm Buckwheat Muffins (see page 165) or Whole-Wheat English Muffins (see page 187).

2 pounds boysenberries

½ cup water

2 tablespoons lemon juice

1½ cups sugar

1½ tablespoons raspberry eau de vie

Combine boysenberries with water in a heavy, non-reactive 5-quart pan. Cover and bring to a boil. Uncover and simmer for 10 minutes.

Add the lemon juice, then begin adding sugar ½ cup at a time, allowing the mixture to return to a boil before adding more. Continue to cook the jam over medium-low heat for another 12 to 15 minutes, stirring frequently. The liquids will reduce, the jam will thicken, and the temperature will rise to 204°F. Add the eau de vie and cook another minute.

Fill the hot, sterilized jars to within ¼ inch of the lip. Wipe each rim clean, attach a new lid, and screw the cap on tightly. Proceed as directed to vacuum seal the jars in a water bath as described on page 20.

Blueberry Rhubarb Jam

YIELD
4 CUPS

Blueberry and rhubarb offer taste and aroma contrasts that cook into refreshing and quite pleasing preserves. They also leave a lovely tangled texture of silky strands and chewy bits in this jam. Grape-Nuts Muffins (see page 166) or Drop Scones (see page 174) would be my choices to serve with it.

1 pound fresh blueberries

1 pound rhubarb

⅓ cup water

½ tablespoon fresh lemon juice

2½ cups sugar

Zest of 1 lemon

Rinse and pick over the blueberries. Trim and rinse off rhubarb stalks. Cut them into ½-inch lengths. Combine fruits in a heavy, non-reactive 4-quart saucepan with the water. Cover and bring to a boil. Uncover and simmer for 10 minutes, stirring regularly.

Stir in the lemon juice, then begin adding sugar ½ cup at a time, allowing the mixture to return to the simmer before adding more. Continue to cook over medium heat, stirring frequently, for 15 minutes. Partially cover the pot to prevent splattering during the last few minutes of cooking. The temperature should reach 212°F.

Fill the hot, sterilized jars to within ¼ inch of the lip. Wipe the each rim clean, attach a new lid, and screw the cap on tightly. Proceed as directed to vacuum seal the jars in a water bath as described on page 20.

Peach Pineapple Jam

Here is another jam in which one fruit with good acidity and an assertive texture—in this case, the pineapple—flatters the flavor and aroma of a sweet but retiring partner, the peach. This preserve offers the palate such an interesting texture and slightly tart finish that a bread with firm or contrasting texture would be welcome. Try one of the English Muffin recipes (see page 186), Butter Pecan Muffins (see page 162), or Tea Brack (see page 171).

- **1¼** pounds whole peaches
- **2** tablespoons fresh lemon juice, divided
- **¾** pound peeled and cored fresh pineapple
- **1½** cups sugar

Dip the peaches in boiling water for 30 seconds, then move them to an ice water bath. When cool enough to handle, peel, halve, and pit them. Coarsely chop peaches and place them in a heavy, non-reactive 5-quart pan. Stir in 1 tablespoon lemon juice to prevent discoloration.

Coarsely chop the pineapple before combining it with the peaches in the saucepan. Cover and bring fruits to a boil. Uncover and simmer 10 minutes, stirring regularly. After most of the fruit juices have evaporated, stir in remaining lemon juice and begin adding the sugar ½ cup at a time. Allow jam to return to the simmer between additions. Cook another 5 minutes over medium heat or until the candy thermometer reads 210°F.

Fill the hot, sterilized jars to within ¼ inch of the lip. Wipe each rim clean, attach a new lid, and screw the cap on tightly. Proceed as directed to vacuum seal the jars in a water bath as described on page 20.

Nectarine Orange Jam

YIELD

5 CUPS

High acidity in both nectarines and oranges makes this a zesty preserve. The cooling effects of fresh mint are especially pleasing here. Grape-Nuts Muffins (see page 166) and Cream Scones (see page 172) taste wonderful with it.

4 pounds nectarines (7–8 cups)

4 large navel oranges (1–2 pounds)

½ cup water

2 cups sugar

2 8-inch sprigs fresh mint (optional)

Dip the nectarines in simmering water for 30 seconds to loosen their skins. Move them to an ice water bath. When cool enough to handle, halve, pit, and thinly slice them. Place slices in a heavy, non-reactive 8-quart pan.

Remove the zest from 2 oranges with a zester (illustrated on page 16), and add it to the pan. Cut the peels from all the oranges and discard them. Halve the oranges and thinly slice them, removing seeds. Add oranges and water to the nectarines. Cover the pan and bring to a boil. Uncover and simmer until juices are reduced, stirring occasionally. Lower heat if necessary to prevent fruit from sticking to the bottom of the pan. (The mixture will reduce to 6 cups.)

Begin adding sugar ½ cup at a time, allowing the mixture to return to the boil between additions. Continue cooking until the jam thickens and heats to 212°F, about 10 to 12 minutes. Stir frequently but keep the pan partially covered to prevent spatters from escaping.

Pour the jam into a 2-quart measure. Submerge the mint sprigs tied with twine. Crush the mint against the side of the container, and let it steep for 5 minutes. Remove the mint.

Fill the hot, sterilized jars to within ¼ inch of the lip. Wipe each rim clean, attach a new lid, and screw the cap on tightly. Proceed as directed to vacuum seal the jars in a water bath as described on page 20.

Ginger Peach Jam

YIELD
4 CUPS

Fresh gingerroot creates just the right exotic perfume and hot sensation on the tongue to provide a memorable accent for sweet peaches. After all, we say "it's ginger peachy" only when everything is just right. This is a jam to savor with English Muffins (see page 186) or Cornmeal Muffins (see page 160).

3 pounds peaches (6 medium)

3 slices fresh gingerroot (size of a quarter)

1 tablespoon fresh lemon juice

⅓ cup water

2 cups sugar

⅓ cup crystallized ginger (1½ ounces)

Dip the peaches in simmering water for 30 seconds, then submerge them in an iced water bath. When cool enough to handle, peel, halve, and remove pits. Finely chop each peach half by hand or with rapid pulses in a food processor.

Combine peaches with ginger slices, lemon juice, and water in a deep, non-reactive 5-quart saucepan or stock pot. Cover and bring fruit to a boil. Uncover and simmer for 10 minutes. Begin adding sugar ½ cup at a time, allowing the mixture to regain the simmer before adding more.

Continue to simmer the jam, stirring frequently, until the jam thickens and liquids reduce. The temperature on a candy thermometer should rise to 212°F and volume reduce to about 4 cups. Keep the pan partially covered near the end to avoid spatters.

Cut the crystallized ginger into pea-sized pieces. After skimming foam off the jam and removing the ginger slices, fold in the crystallized ginger pieces.

Fill the hot, sterilized jars to within ¼ inch of the lip. Wipe each rim clean, attach a new lid, and screw the cap on tightly. Proceed as directed to vacuum seal the jars in a water bath as described on page 20.

Strawberry Kiwifruit Jam

YIELD
2 CUPS

1 pint strawberries

3 large kiwifruit

¼ cup water

½ cup sugar

Rinse, stem, and halve the strawberries. Peel, quarter, and thickly slice the kiwifruit. Combine both fruits and water in a heavy, non-reactive 4-quart saucepan. Cover the pan and bring fruit to a boil. Uncover and simmer for 10 minutes. Add the ½ cup sugar and cook until the liquid is reduced and the jam is thick, about 5 minutes.

Fill the hot, sterilized jars to within ¼ inch of the lip. Wipe each rim clean, attach a new lid, and screw the cap on tightly. Proceed as directed to vacuum seal the jars in a water bath as described on page 20.

VARIATIONS

Cinnamon Strawberry Kiwifruit Jam

Add one 4-inch cinnamon stick to the pan while cooking the jam. Remove before filling jars.

Strawberry Kiwifruit Jam with Vanilla

Split ½ of a large vanilla bean. Scrape out the seeds, and add both the seeds and pod to the pan while cooking the jam. Remove the bean pieces before filling the jars. Alternatively, omit the vanilla bean half and stir ½ tablespoon of vanilla paste into the completed jam.

Strawberry Kiwifruit Jam with Mint

Add 2, 4-inch stems of fresh spearmint to the completed jam. Crush the stems and leaves on the bottom of the hot pan. Let the herb steep with the jam for 5 minutes. Remove the stems and proceed to fill the jars.

Nectarine Plum Jam
with Ginger

YIELD
2 CUPS

1 pound nectarines (3 cups sliced)

1 pound red plums (2½ cups chopped)

⅓ cup water

2 slices gingerroot

1 cup sugar

Rinse, pit, and thinly slice the nectarines. Pit and chop the plums. Combine them with water and ginger slices in a non-reactive 4-quart saucepan. Cover the pan and bring mixture to a boil. Uncover and simmer for 10 minutes, stirring frequently, until most of the moisture has evaporated.

Add sugar ½ cup at a time, waiting for the liquid to regain the boil before adding more. Cook over medium heat for another 5 minutes, stirring frequently, until the mixture thickens. Remove ginger slices.

Fill the hot, sterilized jars to within ¼ inch of the lip. Wipe each rim clean, attach a new lid, and screw the cap on tightly. Proceed as directed to vacuum seal the jars in a water bath as described on page 20.

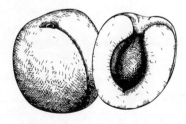

Strawberry Blackberry Jam

YIELD
3½ CUPS

1½ pounds strawberries

1 pound blackberries

⅓ cup water

½ cup sugar

Rinse, stem, and halve the strawberries. Rinse and drain the blackberries. Combine them with water in a 4-quart non-reactive saucepan. Cover the pan and bring mixture to a boil. Uncover and simmer for 10 minutes. Add sugar and continue to simmer another 5 minutes, stirring more frequently as the jam thickens.

Fill the hot, sterilized jars to within ¼ inch of the lip. Wipe each rim clean, attach a new lid, and screw the cap on tightly. Proceed as directed to vacuum seal the jars in a water bath as described on page 20.

No-Sugar Jams

A FRUIT JAM COOKED WITHOUT sugar may sound like a contradiction until you consider the fact that fruit contains its own simple sugar, fructose. This natural sugar in fruits and berries compensates for the lack of sucrose up to a point. The following jams rely on complementary fruit combinations and unsweetened frozen fruit juice concentrates to add natural sweetness rather than resorting to artificial sweeteners. The addition of herbs and spices also enhances their appeal.

The absence of sucrose in these jams leaves them with less shine and a slightly sour finish. No-sugar jams are also more vulnerable to bacterial growth, but that is easily remedied by vacuum sealing them and storing them refrigerated between uses. They are particularly good spread on breads with nuts and raisins, which contribute a natural sweetness.

TECHNIQUE FOR MAKING *No-Sugar Jams*

- Prepare the ingredients for preserving.
- Cook the jams slowly until concentrated, as directed.
- Fill and vacuum seal the preserves as directed.

No-Sugar Peach Pineapple Jam with Apricots

This is a quick, easy recipe, especially if you have a food processor to do the cutting. With such abundant flavor, a light buttery Drop Scone (see page 174) or Risen Biscuit (see page 182) would be the perfect complement.

1 1-pound can unsweetened peach pieces and juice

½ pound dried apricots, finely chopped

1 8-ounce can unsweetened, crushed pineapple in pineapple juice

1 4-inch stick cinnamon

1 tablespoon fresh lemon juice

Drain peaches and reserve the juices. Dice the peaches by hand or chop with rapid on-and-off motions in a food processor. Cut the apricots to the same size. Combine peach pieces with their juice, the apricots, the crushed pineapple with juice, and the cinnamon stick in a heavy, non-reactive 4-quart saucepan.

Bring to a boil, reduce heat to a simmer, and stir constantly until the apricots are soft, almost all moisture is evaporated, and the jam is thickened. This will take about 10 minutes.

Off the heat, stir in lemon juice.

Fill the hot, sterilized jars to within ¼ inch of the lip. Wipe each rim clean, attach a new lid, and screw the cap on tightly. Proceed as directed to vacuum seal the jars in a water bath as described on page 20.

No-Sugar Pear and Blueberry Jam

YIELD

3½ CUPS

This combination draws together fruits from seasons spanning the summer and early fall months. Its flavor is unexpected and delicious. This preserve is a good stuffing for baked apples and is tasty on Apple Cinnamon Muffins (see page 164) or Buttermilk Currant Scones (see page 173).

1 pound blueberries

¼ cup water

1½ pounds Bartlett pears

½ cup unsweetened apple juice concentrate

Combine blueberries and water in a heavy, non-reactive 4-quart pan. Cover and bring liquid to a boil. Uncover and simmer slowly for 10 minutes.

Peel, quarter, core, and dice the pears. Add them to the blueberries along with the apple juice. Raise the heat to medium, and let the pears cook until tender and the juices reduce over a 10-minute period.

Fill the hot, sterilized jars to within ¼ inch of the lip. Wipe each rim clean, attach a new lid, and screw the cap on tightly. Proceed as directed to vacuum seal the jars in a water bath as described on page 20.

No-Sugar
Peach Raspberry Jam

YIELD

3 CUPS

This classic combination works well without sugar when you use canned unsweetened peaches, which are less acidic than many fresh varieties. The raspberries, added after the peaches have been reduced, are barely cooked so their shape and taste remain separate and clear.

Spread this preserve on Zucchini Bread (see page 169) or Butter Pecan Muffins (see page 162) for a real breakfast treat.

2 1-pound cans unsweetened peach halves in juice

8 ounces fresh red raspberries

Drain peaches and finely chop them by hand or with rapid on-and-off motions in a food processor, 1 pound at a time.

Combine peach pieces and juice in a heavy, non-reactive 3-quart saucepan. Cover, bring to a boil, uncover, and simmer until almost all juice is evaporated, stirring frequently. This will take up to 10 minutes. (When the mixture is ready, the bubbles will be small and close together. A spoon scraped across the bottom of the pan will make a hissing sound.)

Off the heat, add the raspberries, tossing them into the hot peaches. Cover the pan, return it to low heat, and continue cooking another 5 minutes. Check the jam and shake the pan rather than stir it to redistribute the berries and juices.

Uncover the pan and turn up heat to medium. Stir gently and occasionally until the jam is thickened again, not more than 5 minutes.

Fill the hot, sterilized jars to within ¼ inch of the lip. Wipe each rim clean, attach a new lid, and screw the cap on tightly. Proceed as directed to vacuum seal the jars in a water bath as described on page 20.

No-Sugar
Apple Grape Jam

Apples and grapes are complementary fruits that hardly ever appear together. Without sugar, their flavors remain naturally tart, and the fresh, spicy gingerroot slices heighten their fruit flavor. Serve Drop Scones (see page 174) and Butter Pecan Muffins (see page 162) with this jam.

3 pounds Macintosh apples

1 12-ounce can unsweetened grape juice

1 cup water

2 slices fresh gingerroot (size of a silver dollar)

Peel, core, quarter, and thinly slice apples. Combine all ingredients in a heavy, non-reactive 4-quart saucepan. Cover, bring to a boil, uncover, and simmer over low heat for 30 minutes or until the apples are soft and the juice is reduced enough to form a jam-like consistency.

Fill the hot, sterilized jars to within ¼ inch of the lip. Wipe each rim clean, attach a new lid, and screw the cap on tightly. Proceed as directed to vacuum seal the jars in a water bath as described on page 20.

No-Sugar
Apple Blackberry Jam

YIELD

3 CUPS

The choice of a tart, firm apple assures this jam a tangy finish and a texture of chunky fruit nuggets. For a sweeter flavor and softer texture, use Macintosh or Jonathan apples.
You could serve this jam with Grape-Nuts Muffins (see page 166) or Tea Brack (see page 171).

- **3** Granny Smith or other firm, tart apples (1¼ pounds)
- **1** 12-ounce can unsweetened apple juice concentrate
- **1** pound blackberries
- **2** 4-inch sprigs of fresh, bruised mint (optional)

Peel, quarter, and core the apples. Dice them coarsely and combine them in a 4-quart pan with the apple juice concentrate. Cover the pot, bring juice to a boil, uncover, and maintain a slow simmer for 10 minutes.

Add the blackberries to the pan. Return the heat to a simmer, cover, and cook for 5 minutes. Uncover, turn the heat up to medium-high, and begin to actively reduce the liquids. Cook until a spoon drawn across the bottom of the pan causes a hissing sound. This will happen within 10 minutes.

Crush the mint stems and add them to the hot jam, off the heat. Steep for 5 minutes or until their scent is noticeable. Remove mint and fill hot, sterilized jars to within ¼ inch of the lip. Wipe each rim clean, attach a new lid, and screw the cap on tightly. Proceed as directed to vacuum seal the jars in a water bath as described on page 20.

No-Sugar Cinnamon Nectarine Jam with Pineapple

YIELD
4½ CUPS

Combined and reduced with pineapple juice, nectarines attain an intense sweet-sour balance. The cinnamon fragrance seems to sweeten this jam. Butter Pecan Muffins (see page 162), Cream Scones (see page 172), and Risen Biscuits (see page 182) are all excellent with it. This flavor will also make a refreshing sorbet if you merely dilute it with Simple Syrup (see page 212) and freeze it on a sheet-cake pan (see page 194 for Fruit Sorbet recipe).

3 pounds fresh nectarines

3 6-ounce cans unsweetened pineapple juice

1 cinnamon stick

Rinse and cut the flesh from the nectarines with skin attached. Cut into ½-inch dice. Combine nectarine pieces with pineapple juice and cinnamon in a heavy, non-reactive 4-quart saucepan. Cover and bring the liquid to a boil, then uncover and simmer over medium heat until the jam has thickened. This will take 15 to 20 minutes. As the mixture reduces, begin to stir more frequently to prevent sticking.

Off the heat, remove cinnamon stick. Fill the hot, sterilized jars to within ¼ inch of the lip. Wipe each rim clean, attach a new lid, and screw the cap on tightly. Proceed as directed to vacuum seal the jars in a water bath as described on page 20.

No-Sugar Pineapple Raspberry Jam with Apricots

YIELD

3 CUPS

The concentrated sweetness of dried apricots is the catalyst in this combination, balancing the acidity of both of the other fruits. An excellent way to savor the sweet-sour taste harmony and complex texture of this jam is on Cream Scones (see page 172) or Risen Biscuits (see page 182).

- **2** cups unsweetened pineapple juice
- **12** ounces fresh red raspberries
- **6** ounces dried apricots, finely chopped

Combine the pineapple juice, half the raspberries, and all the apricot pieces in a deep, heavy, non-reactive 4-quart saucepan. Cover the pan and bring to a boil. Uncover and simmer over medium-low heat until almost all the liquid has evaporated, about 10 minutes. Add remaining raspberries. Lower heat, cover the pan, and stew whole berries gently for 5 minutes. Gently shake the pan to determine moisture level, but do not stir. Mixture is ready when almost all moisture has evaporated, about 5 minutes.

Fill the hot, sterilized jars to within ¼ inch of the lip. Wipe each rim clean, attach a new lid, and screw the cap on tightly. Proceed as directed to vacuum seal the jars in a water bath as described on page 20.

No-Sugar
Blueberry Orange Jam

YIELD
3½ CUPS

In this recipe, whole blueberries retain their watery sweetness as a distinct, refreshing contrast to the acidic tang of the oranges. This jam is delicious on Oatmeal Muffins (see page 163) and Zucchini Bread (see page 169).

3 navel oranges

1 12-ounce can unsweetened orange juice concentrate

1 pound fresh blueberries

Remove the zest from the oranges with a zester (illustrated on page 16). Cut off and discard the inner white peel. Thinly slice the oranges.

Combine juice concentrate, zest, and orange slices in a heavy, non-reactive 4-quart saucepan. Cover and bring to a boil. Uncover and cook on medium-high until most of the liquid is evaporated, 5 to 10 minutes.

Off the heat, stir in the blueberries. Cover, reduce the heat to low, and simmer the jam 5 minutes. Uncover and raise the heat. Cook another minute or two, stirring continuously until mixture thickens.

Fill the hot, sterilized jars to within ¼ inch of the lip. Wipe each rim clean, attach a new lid, and screw the cap on tightly. Proceed as directed to vacuum seal the jars in a water bath as described on page 20.

No-Sugar
Pear and Grape Jam

YIELD

2 CUPS

This variation of the Pear and Grape Preserves (see page 152) has a formidable history. Pear and grape juice, raisoné, as it is called in France, has been made by farmers in Burgundy for several hundred years. A recipe for it first appeared in A. A. Parmentier's early nineteenth-century cookbook in response to a request by Napoleon I for the development of sugar-free foods. (France at that time was being cut off from its sugar supply by an English naval blockade.)

3 pounds ripe Bartlett pears

1 12-ounce can unsweetened grape juice concentrate

Peel, quarter, and core the pears. Thinly slice the pears and combine with juice concentrate in a heavy, non-reactive 4-quart pan. Cover the pan and bring liquid to a simmer. Uncover and simmer for about 30 minutes, until thickened.

Fill the hot, sterilized jars to within ¼ inch of the lip. Wipe each rim clean, attach a new lid, and screw the cap on tightly. Proceed as directed to vacuum seal the jars in a water bath as described on page 20.

No-Sugar
Orange Fig Jam

YIELD

2½ CUPS

This jam blends intensely sweet dried figs with tart orange juice concentrate and barely cooked fresh orange sections. Drop Scones (see page 174) fresh off the griddle or warm Butter Pecan Muffins (see page 162) taste wonderful with this jam.

8 large dried figs (6 ounces)

1 12-ounce can frozen unsweetened orange juice concentrate

3 navel oranges (1½ pounds)

Remove tough stem tips of figs and chop them into ¼-inch dice. Combine them in a heavy, non-reactive 4-quart saucepan with the juice concentrate. Cover the pan and bring to a boil. Uncover and cook at a simmer until the mixture thickens, 5 to 10 minutes. Stir steadily after the first 3 minutes. When jam is thick enough, rising bubbles will come to the surface with plopping sounds. Remove pan from the heat.

Remove and discard the peel from the oranges. Cut down between the membrane and the pulp to release each segment, discarding the membrane. Stir orange pieces into the hot jam. Simmer for another 5 minutes until the jam thickens again.

Fill the hot, sterilized jars to within ¼ inch of the lip. Wipe each rim clean, attach a new lid, and screw the cap on tightly. Proceed as directed to vacuum seal the jars in a water bath as described on page 20.

No-Sugar
Orange Pineapple Jam

YIELD
3 CUPS

Cloves and allspice berries flatter and tame the acid notes in this fruit combination, but you can experiment with other spices as well. Banana Bran Muffins (see page 167) and Oatmeal Muffins (see page 163) are good complements to this preserve. It is also very refreshing when diluted with Simple Syrup (see page 212) or frozen as a fruit sorbet (see page 194).

- **3** pounds navel oranges (4 cups peeled and coarsely chopped)
- **1** 12-ounce can frozen unsweetened pineapple-orange juice concentrate
- **2** cups crushed pineapple, after draining
- **3** whole cloves
- **4** whole allspice berries

Combine all fruit ingredients in a heavy, non-reactive 5-quart saucepan. Tie spices in a piece of cloth with cotton twine and stir them into the pan. Cover and bring mixture to a boil. Uncover and simmer, stirring more frequently as the jam thickens, for as long as 20 minutes.

Off the heat, remove spices and fill the hot, sterilized jars to within ¼ inch of the lip. Wipe each rim clean, attach a new lid, and screw the cap on tightly. Proceed as directed to vacuum seal the jars in a water bath as described on page 20.

No-Sugar Apple Strawberry Jam

YIELD
4 CUPS

The addition of sweet woodruff, with its fresh scent of newly mown hay, adds complexity to this spring jam. A bag of chamomile tea is a good substitute. It will carry a sunlit meadow scent to complement the strawberries. This fragrant jam will add interest and texture to Butter Pecan Muffins (see page 162) or Grape-Nuts Muffins (see page 166).

3 Golden Delicious apples

1 12-ounce can unsweetened apple juice concentrate

4 cups strawberries (1 pint)

5 4-inch sprigs of sweet woodruff or 1 bag chamomile tea

Peel, quarter, and core the apples. Dice them and combine them in a heavy, non-reactive 4-quart saucepan with the apple juice concentrate. Cover the pan and bring to a boil. Uncover and simmer for 10 minutes. Rinse, stem, and quarter the strawberries. Add them to the pan. Return jam to a simmer, cover, and cook for 5 minutes.

Uncover the pan, turn up the heat to medium-high, and begin to actively reduce the liquid. Cook until a spoon drawn across the bottom of the pan causes a hissing sound. This will happen within 10 minutes.

Off the heat, crush the woodruff stems and add them or the bag of chamomile tea to the hot jam. Steep for 5 minutes. Remove the woodruff or tea bag. Fill the hot, sterilized jars to within ¼ inch of the lip. Wipe each rim clean, attach a new lid, and screw the cap on tightly. Proceed as directed to vacuum seal the jars in a water bath as described on page 20.

No-Sugar Kiwifruit Pear Jam

YIELD
2½ CUPS

1 pound kiwifruit (2½ cups)

4 ounces dried pears (¾ cup)

8 ounces Golden Delicious apples (1⅔ cups)

½ cup water

Peel, quarter, and thinly slice the kiwifruit. Dice the pears. Peel, core, and chop the apple. Combine all the fruit pieces and water in a heavy 5-quart, non-reactive saucepan. Cover and bring mixture to a boil. Uncover and cook at a simmer for 10 minutes. Raise the heat and cook another 2 to 3 minutes, stirring frequently to prevent sticking.

Fill the hot, sterilized jars to within ¼ inch of the lip. Wipe each rim clean, attach a new lid, and screw the cap on tightly. Proceed as directed to vacuum seal the jars in a water bath as described on page 20.

No-Sugar
Strawberry Pineapple Jam

YIELD
3 CUPS

1 1-pound can crushed pineapple in unsweetened juice
½ vanilla bean or ½ tablespoon vanilla paste
1 pound fresh strawberries (3⅓ cups)

Pour the pineapple pieces and their juice into a heavy, non-reactive 4-quart saucepan. Score the vanilla bean and scrape out the seeds. Add seeds and bean to the pan. Cover and bring the mixture to a boil. Uncover and simmer for 5 minutes or until most of the juices have evaporated.

Rinse, stem, and quarter the strawberries. Add the berries to the pan, cover, and return the mixture to a boil. Uncover and simmer for 5 to 10 minutes to reduce juices, stirring more near the end of the reduction process to prevent sticking.

Off the heat, remove the vanilla bean or stir in the vanilla paste. Fill the hot, sterilized jars to within ¼ inch of the lip. Wipe each rim clean, attach a new lid, and screw the cap on tightly. Proceed as directed to vacuum seal the jars in a water bath as described on page 20.

No-Sugar Apple Raspberry Jam

YIELD
4 CUPS

- **1** pound Golden Delicious apples (3⅔ cups)
- **1** 6-ounce can unsweetened apple juice
- **2** ounces dried apple rings
- **1** pound red raspberries

Wash, rinse, and wipe dry the apples. Quarter, core, and dice them. Combine the apple pieces with apple juice in a heavy, non-reactive 5-quart saucepan. Cover and bring the mixture to a boil. Uncover and simmer for 5 minutes. Chop up the dried apple rings and add them to the pan. Cook, stirring frequently, until most of the liquid has reduced.

Rinse the raspberries and stir them into the pan. Cover the pan and bring contents to a boil. Uncover and continue to cook at an active simmer for 3 more minutes or until the jam has thickened, stirring frequently.

Fill the hot, sterilized jars to within ¼ inch of the lip. Wipe each rim clean, attach a new lid, and screw the cap on tightly. Proceed as directed to vacuum seal the jars in a water bath as described on page 20.

CHAPTER

5

Jellies

THE ABILITY FOR THE HOME COOK TO understand why jelly jells is the result of a relatively modern chemical discovery. The French chemist Henri Braconnot was the first to isolate pectin in his laboratory in 1825. Before then, preservers relied on traditional recipes, anecdotal evidence, and word-of-mouth to make jelly from high-pectin fruits and berries. A full century later, in 1925, Certo introduced a powdered pectin to the market. This pectin was extracted from citrus fruit and required more sugar by volume than fruit to produce a jell.

Artisan preserving, on the other hand, has relied on the naturally abundant pectin in green apples to promote the jell. Apple's pectin creates a jell with gem-like clarity, that wobbles invitingly when plopped on warm toast and melts smoothly in the mouth, releasing a flood of sweet with sour flavors on the tongue. It's an experience that causes the most harried diner to slow down and savor.

Fruits and berries with high pectin levels jell quickly when juices, sugar, and lemon juice are in balance. The juices of fruits with moderate and modest levels are reduced to concentrate their pectin. Wine and pepper-based jellies rely on the addition of melted Apple Jelly (see page 92).

All jelly recipes call for first cooking fruit in water, straining the juice, and reducing it until it passes the pectin test (diagram of testing for pectin on page 12). High-pectin juice, when boiled with an equal volume of sugar and lemon juice, will form a jell within 10 minutes.

TECHNIQUE FOR MAKING *Jelly*

FRUIT AND BERRY JELLIES

- Prepare fruit for cooking: coarsely chop larger fruits; remove stems, leaves, and stalks but include cores, pits, or seeds.
- Cook fruit for 30 minutes, or as indicated, then strain the juices for one hour.
- Reduce juices as indicated in specific recipes.
- Add lemon juice and sugar to equal the volume of the juices.
- Cook juice to the jell point.
- Skim the jelly, and pour it into hot sterilized jars.
- Vacuum seal the jelly jars as directed.

HOW TO USE APPLE JELLY

- Melt the apple jelly and add lemon juice as indicated in the recipe.
- Add reduced juice or vegetable pieces, boil to the jell point, adding sugar by the tablespoon after 3 minutes if the jell point has not been reached.
- Skim the jelly, and let it sit for 5 minutes, stirring occasionally to distribute vegetable pieces.
- Pour it into hot sterilized jars.
- Vacuum seal the jelly jars as directed.

What do you do when the jelly doesn't set? Check page 21 for first-aid information.

Master Recipe for Grape Jelly

YIELD
4½ CUPS

Homemade grape jelly puts the store-bought versions to shame. It jells easily and has an expansive sweet-sour flavor.

- **4** pounds Concord grapes
- **½** cup water
- **2** tablespoons lemon juice, strained
- **4** cups sugar

Rinse grapes and remove the stems. Combine grapes with water in a heavy, non-reactive 5-quart pan. Cover, bring to a boil, uncover, and simmer for 30 minutes. Occasionally stir and crush the grapes against the side of the pan.

Strain juices from the fruit through a cloth-lined strainer for 1 hour. Measure and reduce juices to 4 cups. Bring grape juice to a boil with lemon juice. Add sugar ½ cup at a time, allowing liquid to return to a boil before adding more. Cook to the jell point. This will take about 5 minutes. Maintain the boil for a full minute after reaching the jell.

Off the heat, skim and fill the hot, sterilized jars to within ¼ inch of the lip. Wipe each rim clean, attach a new lid, and screw the cap on tightly. Proceed as directed to vacuum seal the jars in a water bath as described on page 20.

VARIATIONS

Grape Jelly with Fresh Thyme

Steep completed jelly in a measuring cup with three 6-inch sprigs of fresh thyme for 5 minutes. Remove thyme and proceed to fill and seal the jars.

Spicy Grape Jelly

Tie one 4-inch cinnamon stick, 4 allspice berries, 4 whole cloves, and 3 cardamom pods, crushed, in cloth with cotton twine. Cook the spices with the grape juice as the sugar is added. Remove the bag of spices before filling jars.

Crabapple Jelly

YIELD
9 CUPS

The flavor of crabapples can vary quite a bit from one tree to the next, a fact that makes the quality of your jelly hard to predict even if you use fruit from the same tree year after year. Even then, some harvests are better than others. In fact, one attraction of preserving as an annual ritual is its ability to capture the subtle pulse of nature. It's a pleasure to spread this jelly on a hot Butter Pecan Muffin (see page 162) and watch it begin to warm and soften just as you eat it.

5 pounds crabapples

Enough water to cover crabapples (approximately 2 quarts)

Sugar in the same volume as fruit juices

1 tablespoon of lemon juice per cup of strained fruit juices

Stem and halve the apples unless they are small. Combine them with water in a heavy, non-reactive 8-quart pot. The water should just cover the apples. Cover the pot, bring the water to a boil, uncover, reduce to a simmer, and cook for 30 minutes. Strain the juice through a cloth-lined strainer for 1 hour.

Measure the juice and set aside an equal volume of sugar. Bring the juices to a boil with the lemon juice and stir in sugar ½ cup at a time, each time waiting for the mixture to return to a boil before adding more.

Cook over medium-high heat until mixture reaches the jell point. This may take as long as 15 minutes. Maintain the boil for a full minute after reaching the jell temperature.

Fill the hot, sterilized jars to within ¼ inch of the lip. Wipe each rim clean, attach a new lid, and screw the cap on tightly. Proceed as directed to vacuum seal the jars in a water bath as described on page 20.

Cinnamon Cranberry Apple Jelly

YIELD
7 CUPS

Picture this ruby-bright jelly as a beautiful holiday offering with a stick of cinnamon tied in green ribbon around the jar cap. It will taste delicious spread on any rich brioche breads or Christmas stollen. Tea Brack (see page 171) or Butter Pecan Muffins (see page 162) would be my serving choices from the breads in this book.

2 pounds cranberries

2 pounds Granny Smith or Jonathan apples

6 cups water

Sugar

1 stick cinnamon

Rinse and pick over the cranberries before weighing them. Coarsely chop the apples, removing stems only. Combine fruits in a heavy, non-reactive 5-quart pan. Pour the water over them and bring to a boil. Reduce heat to a simmer, uncovered, and cook for 20 minutes. Strain the juice through a cloth-lined sieve for 1 hour.

Measure the volume of the juice and set aside an equal volume of sugar. Add the cinnamon stick and bring to a boil in a heavy, 5-quart non-reactive pan. Add the sugar ½ cup at a time, returning liquid to a boil each time before adding more. Let the juice boil until it reaches the jell point. This will take about 5 minutes. Maintain the boil for a full minute after reaching the jell point.

Off the heat, remove the cinnamon stick, skim the jelly, and ladle into hot, sterilized jelly jars to within ¼ inch of the lip. Wipe the rims clean, attach new lids, and screw caps on tightly. Proceed as directed to vacuum seal the jars in a water bath as described on page 20.

Black Raspberry Jelly

YIELD
3 CUPS

This luxurious jelly will flatter any bread or biscuit, particularly a chewy English Muffin (see page 186).

4 pints black raspberries (3 pounds)

½ cup water

3 cups sugar

1 tablespoon fresh lemon juice

Pick over and rinse the berries. Combine them with water in a heavy, non-reactive 5-quart saucepan. Cover and bring to a boil. Simmer, partially covered, for 10 minutes, stirring and crushing the berries against the side of the pan. Strain the juice through a cloth for 2 hours.

Measure the berry juice and reduce to 3 cups or add water to measure 3 cups. Bring juice to a boil in a heavy, non-reactive 5-quart pan. Add the lemon juice, then the sugar ½ cup at a time, allowing the liquid to return to a boil each time before adding more. Let the liquid boil until it reaches the jell point.

Off the heat, skim the jelly and ladle into hot, sterilized jelly jars to within ¼ inch of the lip. Wipe the rims clean, attach new lids, and screw caps on tightly. Proceed as directed to vacuum seal the jars in a water bath as described on page 20.

Master Recipe for Red Currant Jelly

YIELD
5½ CUPS

This is the quintessential jelly, with its exquisitely tart flavor, bright ruby color, and shimmering jell. It flatters rich breads and muffins as a preserve and makes a great poaching medium and sauce for peaches, pears, and apples. My favorite bread partners for this vigorous jelly are Buckwheat Muffins (see page 165) and Whole-Wheat English Muffins (see page 187).

4 pounds red currants

½ cup water

Sugar in the same volume as the berry juices

Pick over and rinse the currants. Combine them with water in a heavy, non-reactive 5-quart saucepan. Cover and bring to a simmer. Cook, uncovered, slowly for 10 minutes, stirring and crushing the berries against the side of the pan. Strain the mixture through a cloth-lined sieve for 2 hours.

Measure the currant juice, then place it in a 4-quart saucepan and bring to a boil. Stir in an equal volume of sugar ½ cup at a time, allowing the liquid to return to a boil each time before adding more. Bring liquid to jell point. This may take 10 minutes. Maintain the boil for a full minute after reaching the jell.

Off the heat, skim the jelly and ladle into hot, sterilized jelly jars to within ¼ inch of the lip. Wipe the rims clean, attach new lids, and screw caps on tightly. Proceed as directed to vacuum seal the jars in a water bath as described on page 20.

VARIATIONS

Red Currant Jelly with Cardamom

Bouquet garni: 1, 2-inch stick cinnamon; 10 cardamom pods, bruised to expose the seeds. Add the spices tied in a cloth to the strained currant juices. Proceed with the master recipe. Remove spices just before completed jelly is poured into jars.

Sweet and Hot Currant Jelly

YIELD: **3 CUPS**

- **2½** cups red currant juice
- **1** tablespoon jalapeño chile, seeds removed, diced
- **2½** cups sugar

Combine the currant juice with chile pepper pieces in the bowl of a food processor or blender. Pulse for 15 seconds to fragment and infuse the juice with the chile oils. Proceed to make jelly as described above in the Master Recipe for Red Currant Jelly.

Apple Jelly

With a supply of apple jelly, you can make jelly and preserves with low-pectin fruits, berries, and even vegetables. The pectin in the apple will provide the jell, and its subtle fragrance will defer to the scents of other fruits, herbs, and spices. To avoid being caught short, make more than one recipe and store it in a dark, cool place.

4 pounds Granny Smith apples

8 cups water

1 tablespoon lemon juice, strained, for every cup of strained apple juice

Sugar in the same volume as reduced apple juice

Stem the apples and chop them into 8 to 10 pieces, depending on their size. Place pieces in a heavy, non-reactive pot; include seeds, skins, and cores. Pour in the water. Cover the pan, bring to a boil, uncover, and simmer for 30 minutes. Stir the pot occasionally, turning the apples at the top into the simmering liquid.

Strain mixture through a damp, cloth-lined sieve for 1 hour. There will be about 7 to 8 cups of apple juice. Reduce the juices by half at an active simmer. Add lemon juice and begin adding sugar ½ cup at a time, allowing the liquid to return to the boil before adding more. Begin testing for the jell when the liquid begins to coat a metal spoon. Cook to the jell point. This will take about 5 minutes. Maintain the boil for a full minute after reaching the jell.

Fill the hot, sterilized jars to within ¼ inch of the lip. Wipe each rim clean, attach a new lid, and screw the cap on tightly. Proceed as directed to vacuum seal the jars in a water bath as described on page 20.

Apply Jelly Using Greening Apples

YIELD: **4 CUPS**

- **4** pounds greening apples
- **2** quarts water
- **1** tablespoon lemon juice, strained, for every cup of strained apple juice

Follow the directions for Apple Jelly above, but cook the apples and water for only 20 minutes. You want them to exude their juices but not to cook into applesauce.

This apple variety will strain out to about 1 cup juice per pound of apples. There is no need to reduce this stock but test it to be sure. Add 1 tablespoon of lemon juice per cup of strained juice, and set aside the same volume of sugar as there is juice. Proceed to make jelly as described in the preceding recipe.

Apple Purée for Muffins, Waffles, and Pancakes

After straining off all the apple juice, run the pulp and skin through a food mill fitted with a medium-fine screen. The resulting unsweetened applesauce can be refrigerated up to a month and used to flavor baked goods (see page 164).

Chardonnay Jelly

YIELD
2 CUPS

Jellies made from good-quality varietal wines with a fruity scent and good acid, such as cabernet sauvignon and chardonnay, are particularly flavorful. Since the jelling action is provided by the apply jelly alone, you are free to experiment with different flavors. For example, why not reduce a red wine with a bouquet of your favorite spices for a mulled wine jelly? Tea Brack (see page 171), Zucchini Bread (see page 169), and Cream Scones (see page 172) pair well with this tart jelly.

1 bottle (750 ml) French chardonnay wine

1 cup Apple Jelly (page 92)

3 tablespoons fresh lemon juice, strained

Reduce the wine to 1 cup in a heavy, non-reactive 4-quart pan and reserve. Melt the apple jelly in a non-reactive pot, then add wine reduction and lemon juice. Bring to a boil and cook until the mixture reaches the jell point. This will take about 5 minutes.

Fill the hot, sterilized jars to within ¼ inch of the lip. Wipe each rim clean, attach a new lid, and screw the cap on tightly. Proceed as directed to vacuum seal the jars in a water bath as described on page 20.

VARIATION

Cabernet Jelly

Identical to the recipe above with the exception of the wine used. Substitute a bottle of cabernet sauvignon for the chardonnay. Recommended spice mix: 2 cinnamon sticks, 1 star anise, 7 whole black peppercorns. Tie them in cloth for easy removal.

Kir Cocktail Jelly

YIELD
2 CUPS

If you want to transform your favorite wine aperitif into a jelly, plan to experiment with small batches until you get the right flavor balance. This particular combination of white wine and crème de cassis has a delicate grape taste and the aroma of black currants. It is delicious with a Cream Scone (see page 172) or Grape-Nuts Muffin (see page 166).

1 bottle (750 ml) dry white wine (sauvignon blanc preferred)

1 cup Apple Jelly (page 92)

¼ cup crème de cassis

2 tablespoons fresh lemon juice, strained

Reduce the wine to 1 cup in a heavy, non-reactive 4-quart pan and reserve. Melt the apple jelly in a non-reactive pot and pour in the wine, cassis, and lemon juice. Bring to a boil and cook until the mixture reaches the jell point.

Fill the hot, sterilized jars to within ¼ inch of the lip. Wipe each rim clean, attach a new lid, and screw the cap on tightly. Proceed as directed to vacuum seal the jars in a water bath as described on page 20.

Mint Jelly

The warm perfume of fresh herbs in scented jelly will flood your senses with memories of a summer garden. Herb fragrances are evocative but fragile, so I spread this jelly on simple, buttery Cream Scones (see page 172) or Risen Biscuits (see page 182).

1 recipe Apple Jelly (page 92)

3 tablespoons fresh lemon juice, strained

4 4-inch sprigs of fresh mint

Bring Apple Jelly, lemon juice, and mint stems tied in kitchen twine to a boil in a heavy, non-reactive 5-quart pan. Cook until the liquid reaches the jell point, stirring occasionally and crushing the mint leaves against the sides of the pan.

Off the heat, remove the mint, skim the jelly, and fill the hot, sterilized jars to within ¼ inch of the lip. Wipe each rim clean, attach a new lid, and screw the cap on tightly. Proceed as directed to vacuum seal the jars in a water bath as described on page 20.

Sweet Pepper Jelly

The sweet, smoky fragrance of bell peppers blends well with apple jelly in this recipe. It also makes a beautiful jelly, full of swimming bits of bright pepper gems. This is a delicious addition to a late summer picnic with Cornmeal Muffins (see page 160), Risen Biscuits (see page 182), or Whole-Wheat English Muffins (see page 187).

1 cup red and green bell peppers

2 cups Apple Jelly (page 92)

Zest of 1 lemon

2 tablespoons fresh lemon juice, strained

Remove stems, interior seeds, and membranes from the peppers. Mince the flesh and reserve.

Melt the jelly with lemon juice and zest in a heavy, non-reactive 4-quart pan. Bring this to a boil and add the pepper pieces. Cook on high and check for the jell point. One sign of the jell is the disappearance of small bits of undissolved jelly.

Pour the jelly into a glass measure, skim, and let the preserve stand for 5 minutes, stirring occasionally to distribute the pepper pieces throughout the jelly.

Fill the hot, sterilized jars to within ¼ inch of the lip. Wipe each rim clean, attach a new lid, and screw the cap on tightly. Proceed as directed to vacuum seal the jars in a water bath as described on page 20.

Hot Pepper Jelly

YIELD
4½ CUPS

A little hot pepper goes a long way in fragrant apple jelly. To tame this hot jelly, spread it on cooled Cornmeal Muffins (see page 160) or Buckwheat Muffins (see page 165). If there is cream cheese to slather on in place of butter, so much the better.

- **½** cup chile peppers (any mixture jalapeño, serrano, red chilies)
- **2** cups Apple Jelly (page 92)
- **3** tablespoons fresh lemon juice, strained

Halve the chilies lengthwise and remove the seeds, but keep the white inner membrane intact. Finely mince enough chilies to measure ½ cup.

Proceed as directed for the Sweet Pepper Jelly recipe (page 97).

Rosemary Red Onion Jelly

Onions make a wonderful and unusual condiment paired with apple jelly. The preserve tastes fully of onions with a slight sweet finish and the grassy scent of rosemary—qualities flattering to both breads and cold meats. Try this preserve on Oatmeal (see page 163), Buckwheat (see page 165), or Cornmeal Muffins (see page 160) as well as the Whole-Wheat English Muffins (see page 187). It is also delicious served with cold roast pork, smoked ham, and roast beef.

- **½** cup red onion
- **2** cups Apple Jelly (page 92)
- **3** tablespoons fresh lemon juice, strained
- **2** teaspoons minced fresh rosemary leaves

Peel and dice the onion to measure ½ cup. Proceed as directed in the Sweet Pepper Jelly recipe (page 97). Stir in the minced rosemary stems off the heat after the jell point has been reached.

CHAPTER

6

Marmalades

THE FIRST MARMALADE RECIPE APPEARED IN A 1524 ENGLISH COOKBOOK with its Portuguese name, *marmelado*. It was made with the marmelo quince, a hard, astringent fruit that cooks down to a thick, sweet paste with an intense apple scent. Today's marmalades have evolved into shimmering jellies with suspended bits of sweet citrus pulp and bitter peel.

There are competing backstories associated with marmalade. English marmalade became identified with the fiercely bitter Seville orange imported from Spain. Recipes for the bracing condiment were commonplace in the seventeenth century, but the version produced by Scotsman James Keiller and his wife became the standard in the eighteenth century.

A rival history of marmalade links it to Mary Queen of Scots. According to this account, Mary was treated with French marmalade to combat seasickness on a return trip to Scotland from Calais. This condiment became known in her retinue as a pun on her name, "Marie malade," rather than its French name, *cotignac*. Marmalade quickly grew to be a popular restorative during Mary's reign in the sixteenth century. Its ingredients included oranges and medicinal herbs. Who's to say that a tangy preserve containing trendy antioxidants, a French label, and royal connections wouldn't attract a following even today?

This collection of marmalade recipes continues both narratives. The 'Quick' marmalades are intense and can be made in an hour. They retain much of the bitter essence of citrus rind. A majority of the marmalades are cooked twice, a technique that reduces citrus pectin's bitterness and produces a balance of sweet, sour, and bitter tastes. Both styles are highly therapeutic in their ability to delight.

Several recipes explore marmalade's complex flavor in combination with summer vegetables and spices. Ratatouille Marmalade (see page 126), for example, can easily serve as a savory condiment with grilled lamb or pork, or try it in a sandwich with slices of sharp cheddar cheese and ham.

TECHNIQUE FOR MAKING Quick Marmalade*

- Clean and cut up the fruit and peel.
- Measure the fruit's volume and add an equal volume of cool water to it.
- Cook and simmer this mixture as directed in the recipe.
- Add the same volume of sugar to the cooked base, as directed.
- Cook to the jell point.
- Let the finished marmalade sit, off the heat, for 5 to 10 minutes.
- Stir the marmalade occasionally to redistribute the citrus peel.
- Fill jars and process as directed.

TECHNIQUE FOR MAKING Twice-Cooked Marmalade*

- Clean and cut up the fruit and peel.
- Measure the combined fruit and add an equal volume of cool water.
- Add a portion of the inner peel of the fruit tied in cloth when asked to.
- Cook the fruit and water 15 minutes the evening before and leave the base to steep overnight.
- Remove the cloth bag of peels if added.
- Measure the cooked volume. Reduce it if directed in the recipe.
- Add sugar in the same volume as the base, as directed.
- Boil to the jell stage.
- Let the finished marmalade sit, off the heat, for 5 to 10 minutes.
- Stir the marmalade occasionally to redistribute the citrus peel.
- Fill jars and process as directed.

Twice-cooked marmalades are more complex and delicate tasting than the quick variety.

Thirty-Minute
Orange Marmalade

YIELD
4 CUPS

6 navel oranges

Sugar

Halve and press enough oranges to collect 1½ cups fresh juice.

Scrub the skins of remaining oranges after removing labels and brand imprints. Quarter the oranges and roughly chop. Place pieces in a food processor with ½ cup orange juice, and pulse until the pulp resembles a coarse purée. You should have about 1 quart of juice, pulp, and peel.

Combine contents of processor with remaining juice in a heavy, non-reactive 5-quart saucepan. Cover and bring to a boil. Uncover and simmer, stirring frequently, until the mixture is dry. Measure this volume and set aside an equal volume of sugar.

Return orange mixture to a boil and add sugar, ½ cup at a time, continuing to boil until the temperature reaches the jell point. This should take place within 5 minutes. Off the heat, pour the preserve into a 1-quart glass measure to cool for 10 minutes, stirring occasionally.

Fill the hot, sterilized jars to within ¼ inch of the lip. Wipe each rim clean, attach a new lid, and screw the cap on tightly. Proceed as directed to vacuum seal the jars in a water bath as described on page 20.

Quick Pink Grapefruit Marmalade with Vanilla

YIELD
3½ CUPS

1 large, thin-skinned pink grapefruit

Water

1 vanilla bean or 1 tablespoon of vanilla paste

3 cups sugar

Scrub, rinse, and dry the grapefruit. Quarter it, remove seeds, and finely chop with a rapid pulsing action in the work bowl of a food processor. Measure the pulp and combine the fruit with an equal volume of water in a 4-quart non-reactive saucepan.

Score the vanilla bean and scrape out the seeds. Add seeds and pod to the grapefruit mixture. Cover and bring to a boil. Uncover and simmer until reduced to 3 cups.

Begin adding sugar, ½ cup at a time, allowing the marmalade to regain a boil before adding more sugar. Continue to cook until the marmalade reaches the jell point. This will take 5 to 10 minutes.

Pour the marmalade into a quart measure to cool for 5 minutes. Remove the vanilla bean pieces or stir in the vanilla paste and stir to redistribute the peel. Fill the hot, sterilized jars to within ¼ inch of the lip. Wipe each rim clean, attach a new lid, and screw the cap on tightly. Proceed as directed to vacuum seal the jars in a water bath as described on page 20.

Quick Mixed Citrus Marmalade

YIELD
5½ CUPS

1 thin-skinned pink grapefruit

1 navel orange

1 seedless lemon (smooth skinned)

1 lime

Water

5 cups sugar

Scrub, rinse, and wipe the fruits dry. Cut the grapefruit into 8 pieces, removing seeds. Repeat with the orange. Combine citrus pieces in the work bowl of a food processor and rapidly pulse until finely chopped. Halve and thinly slice the lemon and lime. Measure this total fruit base and combine with an equal volume of water in a non-reactive 8-quart pan. Cover and bring to a boil. Uncover and simmer for 20 minutes or until the mixture is reduced to 5 cups.

Begin adding sugar, one cup at a time, stirring after each addition and allowing the mixture to regain a simmer. After all the sugar has been added, continue boiling for 10 minutes or until the marmalade thickens and clings to a metal spoon. This super-thick marmalade will not boil up as much as the thinner ones. The temperature may not reach the jell point, but it will pass the spoon and cold-plate test. Remove from the heat before fruit pieces begin to stick to the bottom of the pan.

Off the heat, pour into a 2-quart glass measure and hold for 10 minutes, stirring occasionally to distribute the peel evenly in the marmalade. Fill the hot, sterilized jars to within ¼ inch of the lip. Wipe each rim clean, attach a new lid, and screw the cap on tightly. Proceed as directed to vacuum seal the jars in a water bath as described on page 20.

Quick Orange Cranberry Marmalade

YIELD
3 CUPS

This preserve makes a memorable sweet-sour filling for a dessert tart garnished with fresh orange slices. You could also serve it as a relish with turkey or ham.

3 medium navel oranges (1 pound)

Water

2 cups cranberries

3 cups sugar

Scrub the oranges and finely chop one in the work bowl of a food processor with a rapid pulsing action. Cut the peel from the other two oranges. Reserve the peel of one orange in a cloth bag and discard remaining peel. Halve and thinly slice the peeled oranges. Measure the chopped orange, orange slices, and orange peel and pour an equal volume of water into a heavy, non-reactive 5-quart pan. Add the chopped and sliced oranges and bag of orange peels to the pan, cover, and bring mixture to a boil. Uncover and simmer for 15 minutes.

Pick over and discard any bruised cranberries before measuring them. Rinse them, add them to the orange mixture, cover the pan, and return mixture to a simmer. Cook for 10 minutes, stirring regularly. Measure and reduce this marmalade base to 3 cups. Remove the cloth bag, squeezing out the juices into the base.

Return the contents to a boil and stir in the sugar ½ cup at a time, allowing the mixture to return to a boil each time before adding more. Continue to cook until the marmalade reaches the jell point. This will take 5 to 10 minutes.

Pour the marmalade into a 1-quart measure and let it sit for 5 minutes, stirring down the fruit pieces occasionally. Fill the hot, sterilized jars to within ¼ inch of the lip. Wipe each rim clean, attach a new lid, and screw the cap on tightly. Proceed as directed to vacuum seal the jars in a water bath as described on page 20.

Spicy Pink Grapefruit Marmalade

YIELD
4 CUPS

2 thin-skinned pink grapefruits

Water

Bouquet garni: 2 star anise, 5 allspice berries, 1 4-inch cinnamon stick

3½ cups sugar

NIGHT BEFORE

Scrub and rinse the grapefruits. Quarter one and thinly slice. Remove the outer zest from the other, using a stripper tool. Cut off and discard remaining peel; quarter and thinly slice the pulp.

Measure the fruit pieces and combine them with an equal volume of cool water in a heavy, non-reactive 5-quart pan. Wrap the bouquet garni in cloth and submerge it in the pan. Cover and bring the mixture to a boil. Uncover and simmer for 15 minutes. Turn off the heat, cover the pan, and leave it at room temperature overnight.

NEXT DAY

Measure the marmalade mix. Return to a boil and reduce to 3½ cups.

Stir the sugar into the simmering grapefruit mixture ½ cup at a time, allowing mixture to return to a boil each time before adding more. Keep marmalade at a boil until it reaches the jell point, which is 8 degrees higher than the boiling temperature measured on your thermometer. This will take 5 to 10 minutes.

Pour the marmalade into a 1-quart measure and let it sit for 5 minutes, stirring occasionally. Remove the spice bag and fill the hot, sterilized jars to within ¼ inch of the lip. Wipe each rim clean, attach a new lid, and screw the cap on tightly. Proceed as directed to vacuum seal the jars in a water bath as described on page 20.

Orange Marmalade I

YIELD
5 CUPS

This is the first of two twice-cooked orange marmalade recipes. I enjoy it most on warm breads with contrasting flavors and scents, such as the Apple Cinnamon Muffins (see page 164) and Banana Bran Muffins (see page 167).

2 medium navel oranges

1 medium lemon

Water

4 cups sugar

NIGHT BEFORE

Scrub and quarter oranges lengthwise. Cut each quarter in half, then halve the remaining pieces. Continue cutting into coarse dice by hand or chop them, using rapid on-and-off motions, in a food processor. Transfer to a measuring cup.

Peel the lemon, halve it, and thinly slice the pulp, removing all seeds. Measure all the fruit pieces and combine them with an equal volume of cool water in a heavy, nonreactive 5-quart pan. Cover and bring to a boil. Uncover and simmer for 15 minutes. Cool to room temperature, cover, and let it stand overnight.

NEXT DAY

Measure the marmalade base, return it to the pan, and boil it until it reduces to 4 cups. Begin adding sugar, ½ cup at a time, allowing it to return to a boil after every addition before adding more. Allow the marmalade to boil until it reaches the jell temperature. This will take 5 to 10 minutes.

Pour the marmalade into a 2-quart measure and let it sit for 5 minutes, stirring down the fruit pieces occasionally. Fill the hot, sterilized jars to within ¼ inch of the lip. Wipe each rim clean, attach a new lid, and screw the cap on tightly. Proceed as directed to vacuum seal the jars in a water bath as described on page 20.

Orange Marmalade II

YIELD
3 CUPS

In this second orange marmalade recipe, much of the bitter inner peel from the oranges and lemons is discarded. As a result, the preserve has to be reduced more before it will jell. The flavor of the marmalade will be delicate.

2 navel oranges
1 medium lemon
Water
2½ cups sugar

NIGHT BEFORE

Scrub the oranges and lemon. Use a stripper tool to remove 15 strips of peel from the oranges. Place strips in a 1-quart measure. Peel all fruit and cut off the remaining inner white pith, reserving 1 cup of this pectin material in a cloth bag. Discard the rest of the peel and pith. Quarter and thinly slice the oranges and lemon, removing all seeds.

Measure the combined peel strips and fruit. Place them in a heavy, non-reactive 5-quart pan with an equal volume of water. Add the bag of pectin-rich pith, cover the pan, and bring to a boil. Uncover and simmer for 15 minutes. Cool, cover, and let mixture stand at room temperature overnight.

NEXT DAY

Remove the cloth bag from the cooled liquid. Squeeze retained juices into the marmalade base. Discard the bag. Measure the marmalade base and simmer until reduced to 2½ cups.

Add the sugar ½ cup at a time, allowing the pan to return to a boil each time before adding more. Let the marmalade boil until it reaches the jell temperature. This will take 10 to 12 minutes. Maintain a boil for a full minute after reaching the jell point.

Pour the marmalade into a 1-quart measure and let it sit for 5 minutes, stirring down the fruit pieces occasionally. Fill the hot, sterilized jars to within ¼ inch of the lip. Wipe each rim clean, attach a new lid, and screw the cap on tightly. Proceed as directed to vacuum seal the jars in a water bath as described on page 20.

Citrus Marmalade with Star Anise

YIELD
4½ CUPS

1 pink grapefruit (¾ pound)

2 medium navel oranges (¾ pound)

1 lemon (4 ounces)

Water

1 tablespoon whole star anise

4 cups sugar

NIGHT BEFORE

Scrub the citrus fruits and cut the grapefruit into 8 pieces, removing seeds. Finely chop these pieces in the work bowl of a food processor with a rapid pulsing action. Cut 16 strips of peel from the oranges and lemon, using a stripping tool. Cut off the remaining peel from these fruits and discard it. Halve the fruits, remove seeds, and thinly slice.

Measure the combined grapefruit pieces, orange and lemon slices, and peel strips and combine them with an equal volume of water in a heavy, non-reactive 5-quart pan. Add the star anise tied in a cloth bag. Cover and bring the mixture to a boil. Uncover and simmer for 15 minutes. Cool to room temperature, cover, and let the mixture stand overnight at room temperature.

NEXT DAY

Measure the marmalade base. Reduce this mixture to 4 cups and begin adding sugar, ½ cup at a time, returning mixture to a boil each time before adding more. Cook until marmalade reaches the jell point. This will take less than 10 minutes.

Pour the marmalade into a 1-quart measure and let it sit for 5 minutes, stirring occasionally. Remove the bag of star anise and fill the hot, sterilized jars to within ¼ inch of the lip. Wipe each rim clean, attach a new lid, and screw the cap on tightly. Proceed as directed to vacuum seal the jars in a water bath as described on page 20.

Lime Vanilla Marmalade

YIELD
3¼ CUPS

1 pound fresh limes

1 vanilla bean or 1 tablespoon of vanilla paste or vanilla extract

Water

Sugar

NIGHT BEFORE

Scrub and peel the limes with a paring knife. Thinly slice the peel pieces. Halve and thinly slice the fruit, removing all seeds. Measure the volume of sliced peel and fruit (about 2 cups), and add them and an equal volume of water to a heavy, non-reactive 5-quart pan.

Split open the vanilla bean and scrape out the seeds. Add the seeds and pod to the pan. Cover and bring to a boil. Uncover, reduce to a simmer, and cook steadily for 10 minutes. Let this cool to room temperature, cover, and let stand overnight.

NEXT DAY

Measure fruit mixture and set aside an equal volume of sugar. Bring mixture to a boil. Add the sugar, ½ cup at a time, allowing the liquid to return to a boil each time before adding more. Boil until marmalade reaches the jell point. This will happen within 10 minutes.

Off the heat, remove vanilla pod or stir in vanilla paste or vanilla extract. Pour the marmalade into a 1-quart measure and let it sit for 5 minutes, stirring occasionally to redistribute the peel and fruit pieces. Fill the hot, sterilized jars to within ¼ inch of the lip. Wipe each rim clean, attach a new lid, and screw the cap on tightly. Proceed as directed to vacuum seal the jars in a water bath as described on page 20.

Lemon Lime Marmalade with Cinnamon

YIELD
4½ CUPS

Limes and lemons offer distinctly different flavors. One cannot be substituted for the other in food or drink without a noticeable alteration in taste. Yet this marmalade proves they are not incompatible. A blend of their unique qualities creates a new and most delicious taste harmony. Lemon Lime Marmalade is delicious on Zucchini Bread (see page 169) and Whole-Wheat English Muffins (see page 187).

2 large lemons

2 limes

Water

Sugar

1 cinnamon stick

NIGHT BEFORE

Scrub the fruits and trim the outer peel from lemons and limes with a vegetable peeler (illustrated on page 16). Cut the peel into thin strips. Cut off the inner white peel from all fruits, reserving the lemon peels in a cloth bag and discarding the lime peels. Thinly slice the fruits and combine with the strips.

Measure the fruit and peel and combine it with an equal volume of water in a heavy, non-reactive 5-quart pan. Add the cinnamon stick and cloth bag of lemon peels. Cover and bring to a boil. Uncover and simmer for 15 minutes. Let the mixture cool to room temperature, cover, and let it stand overnight at room temperature.

Remove the cloth bag and squeeze out juice into the marmalade base before discarding it. Measure the mixture and set aside an equal volume of sugar. Bring mixture to a boil and add sugar, ½ cup at a time, waiting for the liquid to return to a boil each time before adding more. Cook until marmalade reaches the jell point. This will take 5 to 10 minutes.

Pour the marmalade into a 1-quart measure, and let it sit for 5 minutes, stirring occasionally to distribute the fruit and peel. Remove the cinnamon stick and fill the hot, sterilized jars to within ¼ inch of the lip. Wipe each rim clean, attach a new lid, and screw the cap on tightly. Proceed as directed to vacuum seal the jars in a water bath as described on page 20.

Lemon Ginger Marmalade

YIELD
4 CUPS

The dynamic sensations of sweet, sour, and bitter in lemons combined with hot and aromatic gingerroot make this a marmalade that wakes up taste buds and flatters almost any bread. Tea Brack (see page 171) and English Muffins (see page 186) are particularly good with it. This preserve can also be transformed into a spectacular Lemon Amaretto Soufflé (see page 197).

1 pound lemons

3 slices fresh gingerroot

Water

Sugar

NIGHT BEFORE

Scrub and quarter lemons lengthwise. Remove seeds and thinly slice, leaving peel intact. Measure lemon pieces and ginger slices, and cover with an equal volume of cool water in a heavy, non-reactive 5-quart pan. Cover and bring lemon mixture to a boil. Uncover and simmer for 15 minutes. Let the mixture cool to room temperature, cover, and let stand overnight.

NEXT DAY

Measure the marmalade base. Return to a simmer and add an equal volume of sugar, ½ cup at a time, allowing mixture to return each time to a boil before adding more. Continue cooking until mixture reaches the jell point. This will happen within 10 minutes.

Pour the marmalade into a 2-quart measure and let it sit for 5 minutes, stirring occasionally to redistribute fruit pieces. Remove the ginger slices. Fill the hot, sterilized jars to within ¼ inch of the lip. Wipe each rim clean, attach a new lid, and screw the cap on tightly. Proceed as directed to vacuum seal the jars in a water bath as described on page 20.

Citrus Marmalade with Apricots

YIELD
6 CUPS

6 ounces dried apricots

1 thin-skinned pink grapefruit (1 pound)

1 lemon (¼ pound)

1 medium navel orange (½ pound)

Water

5 cups sugar

NIGHT BEFORE

Coarsely chop the apricots and reserve.

Scrub the citrus fruits and strip 15 pieces of peel from the grapefruit and lemon with a stripper tool. Cut remaining peel from the fruits and discard. Thinly slice the fruit. Cut the orange into 8 pieces, and finely chop it in the work bowl of a food processor with a rapid pulsing action.

Combine and measure the fruit slices, citrus strips, orange pieces, and apricots. Place this mixture in a heavy, non-reactive 5-quart saucepan with an equal volume of water. Cover and bring to a boil. Uncover and simmer for 15 minutes. Let mixture return to room temperature, cover, and let stand overnight at room temperature.

NEXT DAY

Measure the marmalade mixture and reduce to 5 cups. Begin adding sugar, ¼ cup at a time, allowing the mixture to return each time to a boil before adding more. Continue cooking until it reaches the jell point. This will take 5 to 10 minutes.

Pour the marmalade into a 2-quart measure and let it sit for 5 minutes, stirring occasionally to redistribute fruit pieces. Fill the hot, sterilized jars to within ¼ inch of the lip. Wipe each rim clean, attach a new lid, and screw the cap on tightly. Proceed as directed to vacuum seal the jars in a water bath as described on page 20.

Red Bell Pepper Marmalade

YIELD
4½ CUPS

A bell pepper's natural sweetness lends a distinctive taste to the blended citrus ingredients. No spices are specified here, but gingerroot or cinnamon, even bay leaves, would make an interesting addition. Cornmeal Muffins (see page 160) and English Muffins with Yogurt (see page 187) would add texture and an interesting scent to this marmalade, eaten warm for breakfast or with soup for supper.

1 large red bell pepper

1 navel orange

1 lemon

Water

4 cups sugar

Optional seasoning: 3 slices fresh gingerroot

NIGHT BEFORE

Rinse pepper. Holding it upright by the stem, cut the sides from the fruit, leaving behind the core of seeds and membrane. Thinly slice these "side" pieces into thin julienne strips.

Scrub, rinse, and dry the orange and lemon. Cut the orange into 8 pieces, and quarter the lemon. Finely chop the citrus by hand or with repeated pulses in the work bowl of a food processor.

Measure the combined pepper slices and orange-lemon mixture. Pour this base, an equal volume of water, and the optional ginger slices into a heavy, non-reactive 5-quart pan. Cover and bring to a boil. Uncover and simmer for 15 minutes. Let mixture cool to room temperature, cover, and let it stand overnight.

Bring marmalade base to a boil and reduce to 4 cups. Stir in the sugar, ½ cup at a time, returning the pan to a boil each time before adding more sugar. Continue to boil until it reaches the jell point. This will take about 10 minutes. Maintain a boil for a full minute after reaching the jell point.

Pour the marmalade into a 2-quart measure, remove the ginger slices if added, and let it sit for 5 minutes, stirring occasionally to redistribute the pepper strips and fruit pieces. Fill the hot, sterilized jars to within ¼ inch of the lip. Wipe each rim clean, attach a new lid, and screw the cap on tightly. Proceed as directed to vacuum seal the jars in a water bath as described on page 20.

Apple and Onion Marmalade

Apples and onions are frequently paired as a garnish for pork, liver, and cabbage dishes. Bundled in a marmalade with lemon and mint, they make a tasty condiment as well. You'll find this textured preserve delicious with Buckwheat Muffins (see page 165) or Grape-Nuts Muffins (see page 166) and as a condiment with cold pork or roast beef.

- **2** lemons
- **2** medium Granny Smith apples
- **1** small red onion
  Water
- **4** cups sugar
- **6** stems fresh spearmint

NIGHT BEFORE

Scrub the lemons. Use a vegetable peeler (illustrated on page 16) to remove the outer, colored peel from the lemons. Slice these strips into thinner julienne pieces ¼ inch wide. Cut off the remaining peel and the white inner pith. Tie these in a cloth bag and reserve. Halve the peeled lemons and thinly slice them, removing seeds. Combine lemon strips and pulp in an 8-cup measure.

Scrub, quarter, and core the unpeeled apples. Thinly slice the quarters. (They may be chopped into coarse dice with rapid on-and-off pulses in the food processor.) Add these to the measure.

Peel and thinly slice the onion. Place the onions on top of the apples in the measuring cup. Combine this mixture with an equal volume of water in a heavy, non-reactive 5-quart pan. Submerge the cloth bag of lemon rinds. Cover and bring to a boil. Uncover and simmer for 15 minutes. Let the mixture cool to room temperature, cover, and let it stand overnight.

Before discarding it, squeeze juices from the cloth bag into the pan. Measure the marmalade base and reduce it over high heat to 4 cups.

Stir in the sugar, ½ cup at a time, waiting for the mixture to return to a boil each time before adding more. Continue to boil until the jell point is reached, usually within 10 minutes. Maintain a boil for a full minute after you establish the jell.

Pour the marmalade into a 2-quart measure. Add the mint stems and leaves tied with string. Crush the mint against the sides and bottom of the container. Let the mint steep in the marmalade for 10 minutes, stirring occasionally to redistribute the fruit and vegetable pieces. Remove the mint and fill the hot, sterilized jars to within ¼ inch of the lip. Wipe each rim clean, attach a new lid, and screw the cap on tightly. Proceed as directed to vacuum seal the jars in a water bath as described on page 20.

Lime Zucchini Marmalade

YIELD
5 CUPS

Slim, firm zucchini no more than 6 inches long are the best for grating into this mild and fragrant preserve. The dark green and white flecks they leave suspended in jelly will be most tender and flattering to the citrus fruits and seasonings. Lime Zucchini Marmalade is a delicious addition to a batch of Oatmeal Muffins (see page 163) or Risen Biscuits (see page 182).

2 small zucchini (8–10 ounces total)

3 limes (½ pound)

Water

1 bay leaf

1 3-inch stick cinnamon

4 cups sugar

NIGHT BEFORE

Rinse, trim ends, and coarsely grate the zucchini. Scrub, dry, halve, and thinly slice the limes. Combine grated squash and lime slices in a 1-quart measure. Combine this base, an equal volume of water, the bay leaf, and the cinnamon stick in a heavy, non-reactive 5-quart pan. Cover and bring to a boil. Uncover and simmer for 15 minutes. Cool this mixture to room temperature, cover, and let sit overnight.

Measure and reduce the marmalade base to 4 cups. Add sugar to the mixture, ½ cup at a time, returning the liquid to a boil each time before adding more. Cook until the marmalade reaches the jell temperature, which is 8 degrees above the boiling temperature measured on your thermometer. This will take up to 10 minutes. Maintain the boil for a full minute after reaching the jell point.

Pour the marmalade into a 2-quart measure and let it sit for 5 minutes, stirring occasionally. Remove the bay leaf and cinnamon. Stir down the fruit pieces, and ladle the mixture into hot, sterilized jars to within ¼ inch of the rims. Wipe each rim clean, attach a new lid, and screw the cap on tightly. Proceed as directed to vacuum seal the jars in a water bath as described on page 20.

VARIATION

Lemon Zucchini Marmalade with Basil

Substitute ½ pound lemons for the limes. Eliminate the bay leaf and cinnamon stick. Stir 2 tablespoons of finely minced fresh basil leaves into the marmalade after pouring it into the 2-quart measure.

Orange Zucchini Marmalade

YIELD
4½ CUPS

Small, tender zucchini sliced into thin rings is as wonderful with oranges as it is with limes in the Lime Zucchini Marmalade. This time the texture is bolder, and so is the taste—after the introduction of tangy sections of fresh gingerroot. Why not try this preserve with Zucchini Bread (see page 169) for more of a good thing?

- **2** small zucchini (2 cups thinly sliced)
- **2** navel oranges (2 cups chopped)
- **1** quart water
- **3** quarter-sized pieces fresh gingerroot
- **4** cups sugar

NIGHT BEFORE

Rinse, trim ends, and thinly slice the zucchini. Scrub the oranges and cut each into 8 pieces. Chop oranges finely by hand or coarsely pulverize with a pulsing action in the work bowl of the food processor. Measure the combined zucchini and orange. Place this mix with an equal volume of water and the ginger slices in a heavy, non-reactive 5-quart pan. Cover the pan and bring to a boil. Uncover and simmer for 15 minutes. Cool to room temperature, cover, and let mixture stand overnight.

NEXT DAY

Measure and reduce the mixture to 4 cups. While at the boil, begin adding sugar, ½ cup at a time, returning liquid to a boil each time before adding more. Continue to boil until the mixture reaches the jell temperature. This will take about 10 minutes. Maintain a boil for a full minute after reaching the jell point.

Off the heat, remove ginger slices. Let the marmalade sit in the pan for 5 minutes, stirring occasionally to redistribute the fruit and vegetable pieces. Fill the hot, sterilized jars to within ¼ inch of the lip. Wipe each rim clean, attach a new lid, and screw the cap on tightly. Proceed as directed to vacuum seal the jars in a water bath as described on page 20.

Citrus and Green Pepper Marmalade

YIELD
2½ CUPS

1 large navel orange
1 lemon
1 green bell pepper
Water
Bouquet garni: 2 cloves, 2 allspice berries, 10 fennel seeds, 1 bay leaf
4 cups sugar

NIGHT BEFORE

Scrub and wipe dry the orange and lemon. Quarter each, remove seeds from the lemon, and cut all quarters in half. Finely chop the citrus pieces with a rapid pulsing action in the work bowl of a food processor. Rinse the pepper and, holding it upright by the stem, cut the sides from the fruit, leaving behind the core of seeds and membrane. Thinly slice these side pieces into julienne strips.

Measure the volume of pepper slices and citrus pulp. Combine this base with an equal volume of cool water in a heavy, non-reactive 5-quart pan. Add the spices tied in a cloth bag. Cover the pan and bring mixture to a boil. Uncover and simmer for 15 minutes. Let mixture cool, cover, and let sit overnight.

NEXT DAY

Measure the volume of the marmalade base. Bring it to a boil and reduce to 4 cups. Add sugar, ½ cup at a time, waiting for the marmalade to return to a boil each time before adding more. Continue to boil until it reaches the jell point. This will take 10 to 15 minutes.

Pour the marmalade into a 1-quart measure and remove the bouquet garni. Let mixture sit for 5 minutes, stirring occasionally to redistribute the fruit and vegetable pieces. Fill the hot, sterilized jars to within ¼ inch of the lip. Wipe each rim clean, attach a new lid, and screw the cap on tightly. Proceed as directed to vacuum seal the jars in a water bath as described on page 20.

Ratatouille Marmalade

YIELD
5½ CUPS

A classic ratatouille blend of zucchini, tomato, onion, and green pepper becomes a rich marmalade balanced between sweet and sour ingredients. The lemons provide a tartness and pectin that is brought into equilibrium by the sugar.

This is a preserve meant for a serious breakfast table or a picnic spread and can be served with steamy hot Risen Biscuits (see page 182) and Buckwheat English Muffins (see page 187). A vegetable marmalade is also good with cold leftover roasts and spicy sausages.

1 cup thinly sliced red onion

1 small zucchini

1 small green bell pepper

1 Italian plum tomato

2 lemons (13 ounces)

Water

6 cups sugar

4 teaspoons fresh lemon juice

NIGHT BEFORE

Slice the onion and coarsely grate the zucchini. Remove stem, seeds, and membranes from the pepper before thinly slicing. Dip the tomato in boiling water for 30 seconds. Cool under running water and slip off the skin. Halve, seed, and coarsely chop the tomato.

Scrub and wipe dry the lemons. Quarter them and remove seeds. Halve the quarters and finely chop them with a rapid pulsing action in the work bowl of a food processor. Measure the combined fruit and vegetable pieces. Place them in a heavy, non-reactive 5-quart pan with an equal volume of cool water. Cover and bring mixture to a boil. Uncover and simmer for 15 minutes. Let mixture cool to room temperature, cover it, and let it stand overnight.

Measure the marmalade base. Bring mixture to a boil and reduce to 6 cups. Begin adding sugar, ½ cup at a time, waiting for the mixture to return to a boil each time before adding more. Add the lemon juice and continue to boil until the marmalade reaches the jell point, which is 8 degrees above the boiling temperature measured on your thermometer. This will take about 15 minutes. Maintain a boil for a full minute after reaching the jell point.

Pour the marmalade into a 2-quart measure and let it sit for 5 minutes, stirring occasionally to redistribute the fruit and vegetable pieces. Fill the hot, sterilized jars to within ¼ inch of the lip. Wipe each rim clean, attach a new lid, and screw the cap on tightly. Proceed as directed to vacuum seal the jars in a water bath as described on page 20.

CHAPTER

7

Preserves

I WAS DETERMINED TO CREATE A NEW kind of artisanal preserve when I began testing recipes for this chapter more than forty years ago. My goal was to suspend whole berries and fruit pieces in a natural jell rather than rely on the traditional method of creating a sugar-saturated syrup or one reliant on commercial pectin. The technique I developed combines the jelly technique with a steeping period adapted from the older-style preserving method.

My hybrid process involves cooking fruit for 10 minutes, then straining and boiling juices with sugar to create a jelly. The reserved cooked fruit pieces are then added back into the jelly to steep. The jelly, with its fruit pieces, is boiled again to the jell point with a tablespoon or two more of added sugar.

The consistency of these jelled preserves varies from firm, when natural pectin is high, to a soft-set jell in the lower-pectin fruits. A "Quick" preserve recipe is one that combines Apple Jelly (see page 92) with low-pectin fruit. It results in a preserve with a consistency that will easily hold its shape on a slice of toast and cascade attractively down a scoop of ice cream in a dish.

Ever since the Romans stored figs in honey, the term fruit preserves has been synonymous with whole or large pieces of fruit suspended in a sugar syrup. The traditional French process described in *LaRousse Gastronomique* is one of multiple poachings. Fruits are cooked and cooled in a sugar syrup so that the juices they exude when heated are reabsorbed as they cool. Repeated cooking and cooling gradually mingles juices and syrup to the point where the density of the juices inside the fruit is the same as that of the surrounding liquid, causing the fruit to hang suspended in the poaching medium. It's safe to say that the oldest technique for making a preserve did not employ a pectin jell.

TECHNIQUE FOR MAKING Preserves

QUICK PRESERVES

- Prepare the fruit or berries for cooking.
- Simmer the fruit for 10 minutes to release the pectin and reduce juices.
- Strain and measure the fruit; melt the same volume Apple Jelly in a saucepan.
- Add the fruit pieces and cook to the jell point, adding sugar by the tablespoon if the jell point is not reached in 3 minutes.
- Allow the preserve to sit for 5 minutes, stirring occasionally, so that the fruit pieces can become evenly distributed in the preserve.
- Vacuum seal the preserves as directed.

PRESERVES

- Prepare the fruit or berries for cooking.
- Simmer the fruit for 10 minutes to release the pectin.
- Strain the juices. Cook to concentrate if indicated. Reserve the fruit pieces.
- Cook the juices with specified amounts of sugar and lemon juice to the jell point.
- Stir the cooked fruit into the jelly and steep for 15 minutes.
- Cook to the jell point with a small amount of lemon juice and sugar as directed in the recipe.
- Allow the preserve to sit for 5 minutes, stirring occasionally, so that the fruit pieces can become evenly distributed in the preserve.
- Vacuum seal the preserves as directed.

Quick Strawberry Preserves

YIELD
3 ½ CUPS

- **2** pounds fresh strawberries, 25% underripe
- **½** cup water
- **2** cups of Apple Jelly (page 92)
- **3** tablespoons lemon juice, divided
- **½** cup sugar, divided

Rinse, drain, and hull the berries. Leave any small fruit whole and halve or quarter large berries so pieces are of uniform size. Place berries and water in a deep, non-reactive 8-quart pan. Cover pan and bring to a simmer. Uncover and simmer for 10 minutes, stirring occasionally to avoid sticking. Strain juices for 10 minutes, and measure. Reduce juices to 2 cups or add water as needed to measure 2 cups. Reserve the fruit pieces.

Add 2 tablespoons lemon juice to the juices and jelly in a 5-quart pan. Bring this mixture to the jell point, adding ¼ cup sugar by the tablespoon if the jell has not been reached within 5 minutes.

Pour the hot jelly over the strawberries and let the mixture steep for 10 minutes. Return the preserves to a clean saucepan, then add the remaining tablespoon of lemon juice and any sugar that remains from the ¼ cup set aside for the last step. Boil until the preserves reach the jell point, stirring frequently, for about 10 minutes.

Off the heat, pour the preserve into a 1-quart mixing bowl and allow it to sit for 5 minutes, stirring occasionally to redistribute the berries in the jelly. Fill the hot, sterilized jars to within ¼ inch of the lip. Wipe each rim clean, attach a new lid, and screw the cap on tightly. Proceed as directed to vacuum seal the jars in a water bath as described on page 20.

Quick Red Raspberry Preserves

4 pints raspberries (1½ pounds)

⅓ cup water

2 tablespoons lemon juice

Sugar

Rinse and drain the berries. Combine them with the water in a heavy, non-reactive 5-quart pan. Cover and bring to a simmer. Uncover and simmer for 10 minutes. Measure the volume of the fruit and juices. Set aside the same volume of sugar.

Return the mixture to a boil and add the lemon juice. Begin adding sugar, ½ cup at a time, allowing the mixture to return to a boil each time before adding more. Continue cooking until the liquid reaches 218°F. This will take 5 to 7 minutes. The preserves will be quite thick and sheet heavily from a metal spoon.

Off the heat, pour the preserve into a 1-quart mixing bowl and allow it to sit for 5 minutes, stirring occasionally to redistribute the berries. Fill the hot, sterilized jars to within ¼ inch of the lip. Wipe each rim clean, attach a new lid, and screw the cap on tightly. Proceed as directed to vacuum seal the jars in a water bath as described on page 20.

Quick Blackberry Preserves

YIELD
3½ CUPS

4 pints (1½ pounds) blackberries

⅓ cup water

Grated zest from 1 lemon

Sugar

Rinse and drain the berries. Combine with water in a heavy, non-reactive 5-quart pan. Cover and bring to a simmer. Uncover and simmer for 10 minutes. Measure the volume of fruit and juices. Set aside the same volume of sugar.

Return the mixture to a boil and add the lemon zest. Begin adding sugar, ½ cup at a time, allowing the mixture to return to a boil each time before adding more. Continue cooking until the liquid reaches 218°F. This will take 5 to 10 minutes. Preserves will be quite thick and sheet heavily from a metal spoon.

Off the heat, pour the preserve into a 1-quart mixing bowl and allow it to sit for 5 minutes, stirring occasionally to redistribute the berries. Fill hot, sterilized jars to within ¼ inch of the rim. Wipe each rim clean, attach a new lid, and screw the cap on tightly. Proceed as directed to vacuum seal the jars in a water bath as described on page 20.

Quick Pear Preserves
with Pernod

2 pounds Bartlett pears (6 cups)

2 cups water

3 tablespoons fresh lemon juice, divided

Apple Jelly (page 92), melted

3 tablespoons sugar

2 tablespoons Pernod

Peel, core, and dice the pears into ½-inch cubes. Combine with water and 2 table-spoons lemon juice in a non-reactive 8-quart pan. Cover and bring mixture to a sim-mer. Uncover and cook for 10 minutes or until the juices have evaporated.

Measure the volume of the cooked fruit and melt an equal volume of Apple Jelly in a saucepan, whisking or stirring until smooth. Bring jelly to a boil, then add the cooked pears and remaining 1 tablespoon lemon juice. Add a tablespoon or two of sugar as needed if the jell point is not reached after 5 minutes of boiling. When the jell point is reached, stir in the Pernod and cook another minute.

Pour the preserve into a glass measuring cup and allow it to sit for 5 minutes, stirring occasionally to distribute the pear pieces evenly in the jell. Fill the hot, sterilized jars to within ¼ inch of the lip. Wipe each rim clean, attach a new lid, and screw the cap on tightly. Proceed as directed to vacuum seal the jars in a water bath as described on page 20.

Quick Pear and Grape Preserves

YIELD
4 CUPS

- **2** pounds Bartlett pears (6 cups)
- **1** cup water
- **1** cup frozen unsweetened grape juice concentrate
- **2** tablespoons lemon juice, divided
- **3** cups Apple Jelly (page 92), melted
- **1-2** tablespoons sugar

Peel, core, and cut the pears into ½-inch cubes. Combine them in a non-reactive 4-quart pan with water, frozen grape juice concentrate, and 1 tablespoon lemon juice. Cover and bring mixture to a simmer. Uncover and cook for 10 minutes or until all the juices have evaporated.

Measure the volume of the cooked pears and melt an equal volume of Apple Jelly, whisking or stirring to reach a smooth consistency. Add the remaining tablespoon of lemon juice and bring the mixture to the jell point, adding sugar by the tablespoon if the jell point is not reached within the first 3 minutes.

Off the heat, pour the preserve into a 2-quart measuring cup. Allow the preserve to sit for 5 minutes, stirring occasionally to redistribute the pear pieces in the jell. Fill the hot, sterilized jars to within ¼ inch of the lip. Wipe each rim clean, attach a new lid, and screw the cap on tightly. Proceed as directed to vacuum seal the jars in a water bath as described on page 20.

Quick Cherry Cassis Preserves

2 pounds pitted, tart cherries (4 cups)

½ cup water

Apple Jelly (page 92)

¼ cup lemon juice, divided

Sugar

2 tablespoons crème de cassis

Combine the cherries and water in a heavy, non-reactive 5-quart pan. Cover and bring to a simmer. Uncover and cook for 10 minutes or until the juice is completely reduced. Measure the cherries and set aside the same volume Apple Jelly.

Bring the Apple Jelly to a simmer, whisking until smooth. Pour in the cherries and 3 tablespoons lemon juice to bring the mixture to the jell point. After 3 minutes, begin adding sugar by the tablespoon and lemon juice by the teaspoon until the jell point is reached. Off the heat, add the cassis and return to the heat to boil for another 1 minute.

Pour the hot preserves into a glass measure. Allow 5 minutes for the mixture to cool, stirring occasionally to redistribute the cherry pieces. Fill the hot, sterilized jars to within ¼ inch of the lip. Wipe each rim clean, attach a new lid, and screw the cap on tightly. Proceed as directed to vacuum seal the jars in a water bath as described on page 20.

Spicy Blueberry Preserves

YIELD
3½ CUPS

Fresh, plump blueberries are so easy to eat out of hand or pop into muffin batter that their flavor potential is rarely developed beyond this point. But they can be rich, tart, and more intensely delicious when cooked in a preserve. The addition of spices further heightens the intensity of their concentrated flavor.

This preserve is wonderful with warm Butter Pecan Muffins (see page 162), Buckwheat Muffins (see page 165), and Drop Scones (see page 174). It also serves as a beautiful and tasty garnish in Blueberry Pecan Cheesecake (see page 206). You will find it equally delicious when frozen in ice cream and sorbet or warmed in a sauce for baked stuffed peaches.

3 pounds blueberries

⅓ cup water

1 4-inch cinnamon stick

Bouquet garni: 2 each: 2-inch strips fresh lemon peel, whole cloves, and allspice berries

3 tablespoons fresh lemon juice, divided

2¼ cups sugar, divided

Pick over, rinse, and drain the berries. Combine them with water in a heavy, non-reactive 8-quart pan. Add the cinnamon and the bouquet garni, tied with twine in a cloth bag. Cover the pan and bring contents slowly to a simmer. Cook, partially covered, for 10 minutes.

Strain the blueberry juices for 5 minutes into a measuring container. Reserve the berries and spice bag in a large bowl. Pour the juices into a clean 5-quart pan and reduce them to 2 cups. Return juice to a boil, stir in 2 tablespoons lemon juice, and add 2 cups sugar, ½ cup at a time, allowing the mixture to return to a boil each time before adding more. Continue cooking until mixture reaches the jell point. This will take 5 to 10 minutes.

Pour the hot jelly into the bowl containing the reserved blueberries and spices. Let them steep together for 15 minutes. Return the mixture to the pan and bring to a boil. Add remaining tablespoon of lemon juice and the last ¼ cup of sugar. Cook and stir frequently for 5 minutes; the thickened preserves should heat to 216–218°F.

Pour the finished preserves into a 1-quart measure and remove the spice bag. Stir the preserves once or twice over a 5-minute period. Fill the hot, sterilized jars to within ¼ inch of the lip. Wipe each rim clean, attach a new lid, and screw the cap on tightly. Proceed as directed to vacuum seal the jars in a water bath as described on page 20.

Blueberry Blackberry Preserves

YIELD

4 CUPS

There are just enough tart blackberries in this preserve to highlight the blueberries' watery sweetness. With its low-key sugar and acid balance, Blueberry Blackberry Preserves flatters a wide variety of breads.

- **5** cups blueberries (1½ pounds)
- **2½** cups blackberries (12 ounces)
- **½** cup water
- **3** tablespoons fresh lemon juice, divided
- **2¼** cups sugar, divided

Pick over and rinse the blueberries and blackberries. Combine them with the water in a heavy, non-reactive 8-quart pot. Cover and bring to a simmer. Simmer, partially covered, for 10 minutes.

Strain off juices for 10 minutes and measure the quantity. Reserve the fruit pieces. Return juices to the pan, and reduce them to 2 cups if necessary. Add 2 tablespoons lemon juice to the simmering mixture, and begin adding 2 cups of sugar, ½ cup at a time, allowing the liquid to return to a boil each time before adding more. Continue cooking until it reaches the jell point. This will take 5 to 10 minutes.

Off the heat, pour the hot jelly over the reserved fruits. Stir well and let the mixture steep for 15 minutes. Return fruit mixture to a clean pan. Add remaining lemon juice and return the preserves to a simmer. Slowly add another ¼ cup sugar. Boil until the thermometer reads 218°F, but cook no longer than 5 minutes. Stir regularly to keep the berries from sticking to the pan.

Pour the preserves into a 1-quart measure and let stand for 10 minutes, stirring occasionally to distribute the berries throughout. Fill the hot, sterilized jars to within ¼ inch of the lip. Wipe each rim clean, attach a new lid, and screw the cap on tightly. Proceed as directed to vacuum seal the jars in a water bath as described on page 20.

Strawberry Preserves

YIELD

4 CUPS

What could be more gratifying than a thick layer of dark, sweet strawberry preserves on a warm muffin or Cream Scone (see page 172)? In fact, Strawberry Preserves complement all breads and double as a tasty sauce on fruit and ice cream.

3 pounds strawberries (9 cups whole and cut berries)

1 cup water

3 tablespoons lemon juice, divided

2¾ cups sugar, divided

Rinse and trim the cap from the strawberries. Halve or quarter larger berries so all are of uniform size. Place berries and water in a heavy, non-reactive 8-quart pan. Cover and bring to a simmer, stirring occasionally to avoid sticking. Simmer, partially uncovered, for 10 minutes.

Strain the juice for 10 minutes. Reserve the berries in a large bowl. Place juice in a clean, deep 8-quart pan and reduce to 2½ cups. Skim foam off the juice, add 2 tablespoons lemon juice, and return to a boil. Stir in 2½ cups sugar, ½ cup at a time, allowing juice to return to a boil each time before adding more. Continue cooking until it reaches the jell point. This should happen in 5 to 10 minutes. Skim the jelly and pour it over the reserved berries. Let them steep together for 15 minutes.

Return the preserves to the pan and bring to a boil. Stir in the remaining tablespoon of lemon juice and the remaining ¼ cup of sugar. Boil for 5 minutes, stirring frequently to prevent sticking. The temperature should rise to 218°F and the preserve thicken and sheet heavily from a metal spoon.

Skim the preserves and pour into a glass 1-quart measure. Allow the preserves to stand for 10 minutes, stirring occasionally to distribute the berries evenly throughout the preserve. Fill the hot, sterilized jars to within ¼ inch of the lip. Wipe each rim clean, attach a new lid, and screw the cap on tightly. Proceed as directed to vacuum seal the jars in a water bath as described on page 20.

Peach Preserves with Raspberries

YIELD

4 CUPS

Peaches with red raspberries is a combination made famous by Escoffier's Peach Melba, which is included in our dessert chapter. To further riff on this theme, try freezing this preserve as a tasty Philadelphia-Style Ice Cream (see page 195) or soft-frozen sorbet (see page 194). But try it first as a spread on Cream Scones (see page 172) or Butter Pecan Muffins (see page 162). These flavors are wonderful together at room temperature.

- **3** pounds peaches (7 cups peeled, pitted, chopped)
- **⅓** cup water
- **1** pound red raspberries (1½ pints)
- **3** tablespoons fresh lemon juice, divided
- **2⅓** cups sugar, divided

Dip the peaches in simmering water for 30 seconds. Submerge them immediately in ice water. When cool enough to handle, peel off the skin. Halve the peaches, remove pits, and chop into 1-inch dice. Pick over and rinse the raspberries.

Combine peaches with water in a deep, non-reactive 8-quart pan. Cover and bring to a boil, then uncover and simmer for 5 minutes. Add the raspberries, partially cover the pan, and continue cooking for 10 minutes. Uncover every 5 minutes to stir and check for sticking.

Strain the peach and raspberry juice for 15 minutes. Reserve the fruit in a large bowl. There will be about 3 cups of liquid. Reduce juice over high heat to 2 cups. Add 2 tablespoons lemon juice and bring to a simmer. Add 2 cups sugar, ½ cup at a time, allowing mixture to return to a boil each time before adding more. Continue cooking until mixture reaches the jell point. This will take 5 to 10 minutes.

Pour the jelly over the reserved fruit pieces. Allow them to steep for 15 minutes. Return the preserves to a boil in a clean pan. Add the remaining tablespoon of lemon juice and bring preserves to a boil. Add the remaining sugar and cook, stirring frequently, until the temperature reaches 215°F, but no longer than 5 minutes.

Pour the preserves into a quart measuring cup. Allow it to sit for 5 to 10 minutes, stirring occasionally to redistribute the fruit pieces. Fill the hot, sterilized jars to within ¼ inch of the lip. Wipe each rim clean, attach a new lid, and screw the cap on tightly. Proceed as directed to vacuum seal the jars in a water bath as described on page 20.

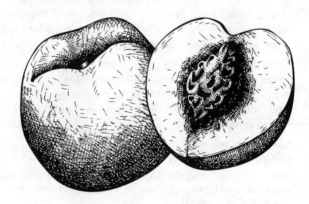

Strawberry Blackberry Preserves

YIELD
4½ CUPS

Why not save a jar of this preserve of succulent summer strawberries and blackberries for a late fall brunch buffet? Surround it with steamy fresh Buckwheat Muffins (see page 165) and textured Grape-Nuts Muffins (see page 166).

- **2** pounds strawberries (6 cups, cut up)
- **1** pound fresh blackberries (4 cups)
- **½** cup water
- **4** tablespoons fresh lemon juice, divided
- **3⅓** cups sugar, divided

Rinse strawberries; hull and cut larger ones in half so they are all of uniform size. Combine them with blackberries and water in a heavy, non-reactive 5-quart pan. Cover and bring to a simmer. Uncover and simmer for 10 minutes. Strain the berry juices for 10 minutes. Reserve the cooked berries in a bowl.

Return juice to the pan and reduce to 3 cups over high heat. Skim the fruit juice, add 3 tablespoons lemon juice, and return to a boil. Begin adding 3 cups of sugar, ½ cup at a time, allowing the liquid to return to a boil each time before adding more. Continue boiling until mixture reaches the jell point. This should take 5 to 10 minutes.

Skim the jelly and stir in the reserved fruit pieces. Allow them to steep in the jelly for 15 minutes. Add remaining tablespoon of lemon juice and return the preserve to a boil. Add remaining sugar and cook for 5 minutes, stirring frequently to prevent sticking. The temperature should rise to 216–218°F and the preserve thicken and sheet heavily from a metal spoon.

Skim foam and pour the finished preserve into a glass 1-quart measure. Let the preserve sit for 10 minutes, stirring occasionally to redistribute fruit pieces. Fill the hot, sterilized jars to within ¼ inch of the lip. Wipe each rim clean, attach a new lid, and screw the cap on tightly. Proceed as directed to vacuum seal the jars in a water bath as described on page 20.

Italian Plum Preserves

The tart flavor and floral fragrance in the skin of this mild plum makes it an interesting fruit to preserve. Zucchini Bread (see page 169) and Oatmeal Muffins (see page 163) are my favorite bread partners for this preserve.

3 pounds Italian plums, pitted and quartered

1 cup water

2 tablespoons fresh lemon juice, divided

2 cups sugar plus 2 tablespoons

Combine plum pieces with water in a heavy, non-reactive 5-quart pan. Cover the pan and bring liquid to a boil; uncover and simmer slowly for 20 minutes.

Strain juices for 30 minutes. Reserve the plum pieces. Reduce juices to 2 cups, add 1 tablespoon lemon juice, and begin adding the 2 cups of sugar, ½ cup at a time, allowing the mixture to return to a boil each time before adding more. Continue cooking until the liquid reaches the jell point. This should take 5 to 10 minutes.

Off the heat, stir the plum quarters into the hot jelly and steep for 15 minutes.

Return preserves to a boil. Stir in remaining tablespoon of lemon juice and 2 tablespoons of sugar. Boil for 10 minutes, stirring frequently to avoid sticking as the liquids reduce and the temperature rises to 218°F.

Off the heat, skim off foam and fill hot, sterilized jars to within ¼ inch of the rim. Wipe each rim clean, attach a new lid, and screw the cap on tightly. Proceed as directed to vacuum seal the jars in a water bath as described on page 20.

Four-Berry Preserves

YIELD
3½ CUPS

Thanks to the importation of commercially grown berries, we now can purchase all these berries at peak ripeness at the same time. This preserve is so rich in aroma and flavor that a warm, chewy muffin of any kind would be a welcome partner.

- **16** ounces strawberries
- **12** ounces blueberries
- **7** ounces blackberries
- **4** ounces red raspberries
- **½** cup water
- **3** tablespoons fresh lemon juice, divided
- **1½** cups sugar plus 2 tablespoons

Rinse, drain, remove green caps, and halve the strawberries. Rinse and drain remaining berries. Combine all four berry varieties with water in a heavy 8-quart pan. Cover the pan and bring to a simmer. Uncover and simmer for 10 minutes. Strain juices for 15 minutes. Reserve the berries in a large mixing bowl.

Reduce the strained juices to 1½ cups. Add 2 tablespoons lemon juice and return to a boil. Add 1½ cups sugar, ½ cup at a time, allowing the mixture to return to a boil each time before adding more. Continue cooking until mixture reaches the jell point. This should take 5 to 10 minutes.

Off the heat, pour jelly over the fruit pieces and let them steep for 15 minutes. Return the preserves to a clean 8-quart pan. Add remaining lemon juice and return to a boil. Stir in the remaining 2 tablespoons sugar and simmer 5 minutes, stirring frequently to prevent sticking.

Pour the hot preserve into a 1-quart glass measure. Let it sit for 5 minutes, stirring occasionally.

Fill the hot, sterilized jars to within ¼ inch of the lip. Wipe each rim clean, attach a new lid, and screw the cap on tightly. Proceed as directed to vacuum seal the jars in a water bath as described on page 20.

Blackberry Ginger Preserves

YIELD
4 CUPS

The dark, toothsome blackberry makes a spectacular preserve, full of sweet-sour contrasts and the fragrance of wilderness. I have added ginger's warm sensations and spicy aroma for emphasis. Enjoy this preserve with buckwheat blinis or muffins.

- **3** pounds blackberries
- **½** cup water
- **2** slices fresh gingerroot (each the size of a quarter)
- **3** tablespoons lemon juice, divided
- **2** cups sugar plus 2 tablespoons

Rinse and drain the berries. Combine with water in a heavy, non-reactive 8-quart pan. Cover and bring to a simmer. Uncover and simmer the berries for 10 minutes. Strain the juices for 15 minutes. Reserve the blackberries in a large mixing bowl.

Measure the blackberry juice and reduce it to 2 cups. Bring the juice to a boil with the gingerroot slices and 2 tablespoons lemon juice. Stir in 2 cups sugar, ½ cup at a time, allowing the pan to return to a boil between additions. Continue to boil until mixture reaches the jell point. This will take about 5 minutes.

Pour the jelly over the reserved berries and allow preserve to steep for 15 minutes. Return the preserve to a clean pan, add remaining tablespoon of lemon juice, cover, and bring to a boil. Add the remaining sugar and cook to the jell point, another 5 minutes or so.

Pour the hot preserves into a 2-quart measure. Remove the gingerroot slices. Let the preserve sit for 5 minutes, stirring occasionally to distribute the berries in the jell. Fill the hot, sterilized jars to within ¼ inch of the lip. Wipe each rim clean, attach a new lid, and screw the cap on tightly. Proceed as directed to vacuum seal the jars in a water bath as described on page 20.

Red Raspberry Preserves

YIELD
5 CUPS

These preserves enhance any breakfast, slathered on an English Muffin (see page 186), and can be very dressy for high tea, spooned onto Cream Scones (see page 172) and Butter Pecan Muffins (see page 162). A look through Chapter 9 will show you how many delicious dessert alliances can be made with raspberry preserve, especially Linzer Torte (see page 208) and Peach Melba (see page 193).

3 pounds red raspberries (9 cups)

½ cup water

3 tablespoons lemon juice, divided

2 cups sugar plus 2 tablespoons

Rinse and drain the berries. Combine with water in a heavy, non-reactive 8-quart pan. Cover and bring to a simmer. Uncover and simmer the berries for 10 minutes. Strain the juices for 15 minutes. Reserve the berries in a large mixing bowl. Measure the raspberry juice and reduce it to 2 cups.

Bring juice to a boil, stir in 2 tablespoons lemon juice, and begin adding the 2 cups of sugar ½ cup at a time, allowing the mixture to return to a boil each time before adding more. Cook until the mixture reaches the jell point. This will take less than 5 minutes.

Stir the hot jelly into the reserved raspberries and let them steep for 15 minutes. Return to a boil. Add remaining tablespoon of lemon juice and 2 tablespoons sugar. Continue cooking until preserve reaches the jell point. This should take 7 to 10 minutes. Boil for an additional minute. Stir frequently during this time to prevent sticking.

Pour the preserves into a 2-quart measure. Hold for 5 minutes, stirring occasionally to distribute the berries in the jell. Skim the preserves and fill the hot, sterilized jars to within ¼ inch of the lip. Wipe each rim clean, attach a new lid, and screw the cap on tightly. Proceed as directed to vacuum seal the jars in a water bath as described on page 20.

Raspberry Red Currant Preserves

YIELD

5 CUPS

Brilliant red currants are a special find at farmers' markets in late June and July. It's worthwhile seeking them out. Their tartness is a wonderful complement to other berries. This jam is delicious with all the breads. My favorites are the Buttermilk Currant Scones (see page 173) and Tea Brack (see page 171).

- **2** cups red currant juice (strained from 2½ pounds red currants)
- **2** pounds red raspberries
- **3** tablespoons lemon juice, divided
- **3¼** cups sugar, divided

Follow directions in Master Recipe for Red Currant Jelly (see page 90) to extract juice from the currants.

Combine raspberries and currant juice in an 8-quart pan, cover, and bring to a boil. Uncover and simmer for 10 minutes. Strain the juices for 15 minutes. Reserve the berries in the sieve. Measure the juice and either reduce or add water to measure 3 cups.

Add 2 tablespoons lemon juice to the strained fruit juices in a clean 8-quart pan. Cover and bring to a boil. Uncover and add 3 cups sugar, ½ cup at a time, allowing the liquid to regain a boil each time before adding more. This will take less than 5 minutes.

Stir the reserved berries into the hot jelly and steep for 15 minutes. Add remaining tablespoon of lemon juice. Cover the pan and bring to a boil. Uncover and stir in remaining ¼ cup sugar. Keep at a boil until the jell point is reached, about 5 minutes.

Pour the preserves into a 2-quart glass measure. Let the preserves sit for 5 minutes, stirring occasionally to redistribute the berries. Fill the hot, sterilized jars to within ¼ inch of the lip. Wipe each rim clean, attach a new lid, and screw the cap on tightly. Proceed as directed to vacuum seal the jars in a water bath as described on page 20.

Blueberry Raspberry Preserves

YIELD
5½ CUPS

This preserve of blueberries and raspberries is a special midsummer treat to serve with warm muffins or scones.

- **2** pounds fresh blueberries (6 cups)
- **1** pound red raspberries
- **½** cup water
- **3** tablespoons fresh lemon juice, divided
- **3¼** cups sugar, divided

Rinse and pick over the berries. Combine with water in a heavy, non-reactive 8-quart pan. Cover and bring to a boil. Uncover and simmer for 10 minutes. Strain juice for 15 minutes. Reserve the berries in a large bowl. Measure the juice and either reduce or add water to measure 3 cups.

Bring juice to a simmer in a clean 8-quart pan. Stir in 2 tablespoons lemon juice and add 3 cups sugar, ½ cup at a time, allowing the mixture to return to a boil each time before adding more. Boil mixture until it reaches the jell point. This will take place within 5 minutes.

Stir the hot jelly into the reserved berries and let them steep for 15 minutes. Return to a clean pan, add remaining tablespoon of lemon juice, and return preserves to a boil. Stir in the remaining sugar and boil until the thermometer reads 218°F but no longer than 10 more minutes, stirring frequently.

Off the heat, pour preserves into a 2-quart measure and allow it to steep for 10 minutes, stirring occasionally to distribute the berries in the jell. Fill the hot, sterilized jars to within ¼ inch of the lip. Wipe each rim clean, attach a new lid, and screw the cap on tightly. Proceed as directed to vacuum seal the jars in a water bath as described on page 20.

Apple Red Raspberry Preserves

YIELD

5½ CUPS

2 pounds firm, tart apples (Granny Smith, Jonathan, or Cortland)

1½ pounds red raspberries

½ cup water

3 tablespoons lemon juice, divided

2¾ cups sugar, divided

Peel, quarter, core, and thinly slice the apples. Rinse and drain the raspberries, and combine them with the apple slices and water in a heavy, non-reactive 5-quart pan. Cover and bring to a boil. Uncover and simmer for 10 minutes. Stir occasionally to prevent sticking.

Strain the hot juices from the fruit pieces for 15 minutes. Reserve the fruit pieces in a large bowl. Juices should measure 2½ cups. Add water if there is less or reduce to that amount over high heat if there is more.

Bring fruit juice to a boil with 2 tablespoons lemon juice and 2½ cups of sugar added ½ cup at a time. Wait for the liquid to return to a boil each time before adding more. Continue boiling to the jell point. This should take about 5 minutes.

Off the heat, stir jelly into the fruit pieces. Let them steep for 15 minutes. Return the preserves to a boil in a clean pan, and add remaining tablespoon of lemon juice and final ¼ cup sugar. Cook for 5 minutes, stirring quite often to prevent sticking. The mixture will be quite thick, and its temperature should rise to 216°F.

Transfer the preserve into a 2-quart measure and allow it to sit for 5 minutes, stirring occasionally to evenly distribute the fruit pieces. Fill the hot, sterilized jars to within ¼ inch of the lip. Wipe each rim clean, attach a new lid, and screw the cap on tightly. Proceed as directed to vacuum seal the jars in a water bath as described on page 20.

Pear and Grape Preserves

Pears and grapes can be cooked with or without sugar with equally satisfying results (No-Sugar Pear and Grape Jam, page 76). Savor this sweetened pear and grape combination on Oatmeal Muffins (see page 163), Butter Pecan Muffins (see page 162), or Drop Scones (see page 174).

3 pounds Concord grapes (3 cups strained juice)

1 cup water

3 pounds ripe Bartlett pears

3 tablespoons lemon juice, divided

3⅓ cups sugar, divided

Rinse and stem the grapes. Cover and bring them to a simmer with the water in a heavy, non-reactive 4-quart pan. Uncover the pan and simmer slowly for 30 minutes, stirring often and crushing the grapes against the side of the pot.

Strain grape juice for 1 hour through a sieve lined with cloth. You should have about 3 cups of juice. If there is less, add water to make up the difference. If there is more, reduce juice to 3 cups. Discard grape skins, fruit, seeds, and stems.

Peel, quarter, and core the pears. Thinly slice the pears and combine them in an 8-quart pan with the grape juice and 2 tablespoons lemon juice. Bring mixture to a boil, regulate heat to a gentle simmer, cover, and cook for 10 minutes.

Off the heat, strain the juice for 15 minutes. Reserve pear pieces in a large mixing bowl. Reduce the juice to 3 cups.

Bring juice to a boil and add 3 cups of sugar, ½ cup at a time, allowing the liquid to return to a boil between additions. Continue boiling until mixture reaches the jell point. This should take 5 to 7 minutes.

Off the heat, stir the jelly into the pear pieces and steep for 15 minutes. Return the preserve to a boil, add remaining tablespoon of lemon juice, and gradually stir in the remaining sugar. Boil until the preserve sheets from a spoon, but no longer than 10 minutes. Stir frequently to prevent sticking.

Off the heat, pour the preserve into a quart measure and let the mixture steep, stirring occasionally to distribute the fruit pieces in the jell. Fill the hot, sterilized jars to within ¼ inch of the lip. Wipe each rim clean, attach a new lid, and screw the cap on tightly. Proceed as directed to vacuum seal the jars in a water bath as described on page 20.

Serviceberry and Wild Black Raspberry Preserves

YIELD
6 CUPS

The serviceberry tree is found as an understory tree in old-forest growth in temperate areas throughout the United States. Its slender, light gray branches and silver-green leaves often take the shape of a spreading shrub, which is quite distinctive. It also has other names, such as shadbush, shadblow, and Juneberry. This last name refers to the small dark purple berries it produces from June into early July.

Although their taste, fresh from the tree, is sweet and bland, serviceberries develop an enticing bouquet of roses when cooked. Except for this trait, you would never guess that the serviceberry is a member of the rose family. Serviceberries have excellent pectin content and form an inspired partnership with wild, scratchy black raspberries that ripen at the same time in similar wooded settings. Try this preserve with English Muffins (see page 186), Cream Scones (see page 172), and Tea Brack (see page 171).

- **2** pounds serviceberries
- **¼** cup water
- **1** pound black raspberries (4 cups)
- **2** tablespoons fresh lemon juice
- **5** cups sugar

Rinse and combine the serviceberries with the water in a heavy, non-reactive 5-quart saucepan. Cover and bring to a boil. Uncover and simmer 15 minutes, stirring and crushing the berries to extract their juices. Strain this mixture for 2 hours. There will be about 3 cups of strained juices. If there is more juice, reduce it to 3 cups. If there is less juice, add water to make 3 cups.

Return the serviceberry juice to a clean 5-quart saucepan. Add the black raspberries, cover, and bring mixture to a boil. Uncover and simmer for 10 minutes. Pour in the lemon juice, then begin adding sugar ½ cup at a time, allowing mixture to regain the boil before adding more. Cook preserve on medium-high heat, stirring regularly with a long-handled spoon, until it reaches the jell point. This will take about 15 minutes.

Cover the pot when the preserve begins to spatter as it nears 220°F. Check the temperature, and stir to reduce the heat every minute or so. Pour the preserve into a 2-quart measure. Let it sit, stirring occasionally to redistribute the berries in the jell.

Fill the hot, sterilized jars to within ¼ inch of the lip. Wipe each rim clean, attach a new lid, and screw the cap on tightly. Proceed as directed to vacuum seal the jars in a water bath as described on page 20.

Apple Grape Preserves

YIELD
4 CUPS

3 pounds Concord grapes (3 cups strained juice)

½ cup water

2 cups Granny Smith or Golden Delicious apples

3 tablespoons lemon juice, divided

Sugar, divided

Rinse and stem the grapes. Combine water and grapes in a heavy, non-reactive 8-quart pan, cover, and bring to a boil. Uncover, reduce the heat to a simmer, and cook 30 minutes. Strain grape juice for 2 hours. Measure and reduce to 3 cups. Discard the grapes.

Peel, quarter, and core the apples. Slice them into thin wedges. Combine the apple pieces with the grape juice and 2 tablespoons lemon juice in a 5-quart pan. Cover the pan and bring to a boil. Uncover and simmer for 10 minutes. Apples will soften but remain whole. Strain juice for 10 minutes. Reserve the apples in a large mixing bowl.

Measure the strained jelly and set aside an equal volume of sugar. Bring juice to a boil and add sugar, ½ cup at a time, allowing juice to return to a boil each time before adding more. Continue cooking over high heat until the mixture reaches the jell point. This should take less than 5 minutes.

Remove the jelly from the heat, pour it over the apple pieces, and let steep for 15 minutes. Return the preserves to a boil in a clean pan. Stir in the last tablespoon of lemon juice and an additional ¼ cup of ⅔ sugar. Let the mixture cook at a boil until it reaches 218°F but no longer than 10 minutes. The preserve will be thick and sheet from a spoon. Stir the pan frequently to prevent sticking.

Off the heat, skim foam from the preserve and pour into a quart measure. Let the preserve steep, stirring occasionally to distribute the apple pieces in the jell. Fill the hot, sterilized jars to within ¼ inch of the lip. Wipe each rim clean, attach a new lid, and screw the cap on tightly. Proceed as directed to vacuum seal the jars in a water bath as described on page 20.

CHAPTER

8

Breads and Muffins

SO OFTEN A RESTAURANT BREAKFAST ANYWHERE IN AMERICA arrives with a disappointing side of dry toast and a tiny plastic container of fruit jelly. Compare that with having your own homemade bread and jam to start the day. It makes getting up in the morning worthwhile.

The baking powder breads and muffins in this chapter are easy enough to make in the morning even before you've had a cup of coffee. If you're not up to rising and baking right away, plan ahead and defrost some you've already baked. This routine will come easily to those who are always thinking about their next meal.

English Muffins (see page 186), French Toast (see page 180), and the Giant Sunday Popover (see page 175) are bigger projects, more suited to the slower pace of weekend breakfasts. They are also a treat to serve to friends for brunch. Risen Biscuits (see page 182) and blinis (page 178) are other good choices.

One final tip for insuring that your homemade jams and jellies have the best bread companions possible is to warm the bread in an oven just before serving. This goes for store-bought and day-old bread as well. You can revive bread by placing it in a 300°F oven for 5 to 10 minutes. The aroma of warm bread has such universal appeal that if you weren't hungry before, you will be by the time it arrives at the table.

BASIC BAKING INGREDIENTS AND PROCEDURES

A few basic rules apply to all these bread recipes despite their technical differences.

- Large eggs and unsalted butter are standard ingredients in all the recipes.
- Replace unbleached flour if it is more than two years old. To keep it for longer periods, store it tightly sealed in the freezer and let it warm to room temperature before using.
- Unless otherwise specified, begin with all ingredients at room temperature.
- Measure dry ingredients in metal cups, fill with a scoop, and scrape flat without compressing.

- Measure liquids in heatproof glass measuring containers.
- Place a mercury thermometer in your oven to verify its temperature before baking. Ovens stray from their calibrated settings over time and need to be checked with a thermometer periodically and recalibrated if necessary.
- Test breads and muffins with an instant-read thermometer to assure that they are done. A reading of 200°F assures that the wheat starch has gelatinized.

BASIC TECHNIQUES

- The techniques for assembling ingredients are designed either to inhibit or to expand the gluten strength of the wheat flour, depending on the leavener.
- The wet ingredients are gradually worked into the dry in all the bread recipes containing baking powder and baking soda. The dough or batter is stirred until the ingredients are just blended. Additional mixing tightens the flour's gluten strands. A cone-shaped muffin top is a sign that a baking powder batter has been over-beaten.
- In the yeast breads, gluten activity is encouraged by pulling and stretching the dough. This kneading activity gives the English Muffins (see page 186) and Risen Biscuits (see page 182) a firm, chewy texture. The Russian Buckwheat Blinis with Blackberry Sauce (see page 178) is the only exception. This dough is too soft to knead and rises naturally over time without encouragement.
- Butter and oil used to prepare baking molds and pans are not listed as ingredients.

Cornmeal Muffins

Here is a muffin recipe that can be modified for almost any occasion. Made as given below, the muffins can be served with a meal or tea and delicate Lime Vanilla Marmalade (see page 113) or Peach Blueberry Jam (see page 43). If you were to substitute brown sugar for white, bacon drippings for butter, a coarsely ground cornmeal, and buttermilk for milk, you would have a Country-Style Cornmeal Muffin (recipe follows). This would call for a jar of zesty Apricot Orange Jam (see page 42) or Damson Plum Jam (see page 53).

- **2** tablespoons sugar
- **3** tablespoons unsalted butter at room temperature
- **¾** cup cornmeal
- **4** large eggs
- **1** cup milk
- **1** cup unbleached flour
- **1** tablespoon baking powder
- **½** teaspoon salt
- **¼** teaspoon freshly ground black pepper

Preheat the oven to 400°F. Butter a 12-muffin tin.

Cream the sugar with the butter in a 2-quart bowl. Stir in the cornmeal, eggs (1 at a time), and milk.

Measure flour, baking powder, salt, and pepper into a 2-quart bowl and whisk until well combined. Make a well in the center and pour the wet ingredients into the dry, stirring until they are just blended.

Pour the batter into the molds and bake for 15 minutes until the muffins are puffed, golden brown, and register 200°F internally on an instant-read thermometer. Let them cool in the pan for 10 minutes. Unmold the muffins and serve them warm with jam or preserves.

Country-Style Cornmeal Muffins

- **2** tablespoons brown sugar
- **3** tablespoons bacon drippings
- **¾** cup coarse cornmeal
- **4** large eggs
- **1** cup buttermilk
- **1** cup unbleached white flour
- **2** teaspoons baking powder
- **1** teaspoon baking soda
- **½** teaspoon salt
- **¼** teaspoon freshly ground black pepper

Follow the directions for the Cornmeal Muffins above.

Butter Pecan Muffins

Usually all one needs to enjoy the rich flavor of steamy, warm pecan muffins is the muffin itself. But by the time a second muffin is on your plate, so is a mild Orange Marmalade (see pages 111, 112) and a tablespoon of Spicy Blueberry Preserves (see page 138). In this case, more is better.

- ¾ cup chopped toasted pecans
- 6 tablespoons unsalted butter
- 3 tablespoons brown sugar
- 4 teaspoons baking powder
- 2 cups unbleached flour
- ½ teaspoon salt
- 1 cup milk
- 4 large eggs

Preheat the oven to 350°F, butter a 12-muffin tin, and toast the pecan halves for 10 minutes. Let the nuts cool before chopping. Melt 6 tablespoons of butter and reserve. Raise the oven setting to 400°.

Measure the sugar, baking powder, flour, and salt into a 2-quart bowl and stir well. Make a well in the center and pour in the melted butter, milk, and eggs. Beat the wet ingredients together and gradually incorporate the dry ingredients. Stir together until just blended. Fold the warm pecans into the batter.

Spoon the batter into the molds and bake for 20 minutes or until the muffins are puffed, lightly browned, and register 200°F internally on an instant-read thermometer. Let them cool in the pan for 5 minutes. Unmold and serve warm with jam or preserves.

Oatmeal Muffins

YIELD
12 MUFFINS

Sometimes you want a bread that will showcase your preserving prowess. An oatmeal muffin offers just the right profile, with its slightly chewy texture and warm, fresh grain scent. Now is your chance to serve that fabulous Black Raspberry Cassis Jam (see page 37) or the exotic Kiwifruit Mint Jam (see page 45) and really wow your guests.

1 cup instant oatmeal

1 cup milk

2 tablespoons unsalted butter

3 tablespoons brown sugar

1½ cups unbleached flour

4 teaspoons baking powder

½ teaspoon salt

4 large eggs

Preheat the oven to 400°F. Butter a 12-muffin tin.

Measure the oatmeal into a 2-quart bowl. Heat the milk and butter to a simmer. Pour this hot mixture over the oatmeal and let it stand for 10 minutes. Beat the eggs into the oatmeal mixture.

Measure and mix together the sugar, flour, baking powder, and salt in a 2-quart bowl. Make a well in the center, pour the wet ingredients into the dry, and stir until just blended.

Pour the batter into the molds and bake for 15 minutes or until the muffins are puffed, browned, and register 200°F internally on an instant-read thermometer. Let them cool in the pan for 10 minutes. Unmold and eat warm with jam or marmalade.

Apple Cinnamon Muffins

YIELD

12 MUFFINS

This muffin can easily become the delicious byproduct of the Apple Jelly recipe (page 92). Simply press the strained apple pieces through a food mill and fold the strained applesauce into the other muffin ingredients. The soft apple pulp gives the bread a moist, delicate texture and cinnamon revives the apple's floral scent. One of the intensely flavorful no-sugar jams would heighten the flavor of this subtle muffin. My choice would be the No-Sugar Apple Blackberry Jam (see page 72) or No-Sugar Pear and Blueberry Jam (see page 69).

3 tablespoons soft unsalted butter

2 tablespoons brown sugar

3 large eggs

1 cup unsweetened applesauce or apple purée (see Apple Jelly, page 92)

1½ cups unbleached flour

½ teaspoon ground cinnamon

½ teaspoon salt

4 teaspoons baking powder

Preheat oven to 400°F. Butter a 12-muffin tin.

Cream the butter with the brown sugar in a 2-quart bowl. Add eggs 1 at a time, mixing each in well. Stir in the applesauce.

Measure the flour, cinnamon, salt, and baking powder into a 2-quart bowl, stir the ingredients together, and make a well in the center. Pour the wet mixture into the dry and stir together until they are just blended.

Spoon the batter into the molds and bake for 15 minutes or until muffins are puffed, browned, and register 200°F internally on an instant-read thermometer. Let them cool in the pan for 10 minutes. Unmold and serve muffins warm with butter and marmalade.

Buckwheat Muffins

YIELD
12 MUFFINS

Watch this muffin raise eyebrows in delight at its rich array of scents and flavors. The buckwheat flour has a slightly bitter tang; the buttermilk is pleasingly sour. Serve an assertive fruit flavor preserve that can hold its own with this robust partner: Plum Jam with Cardamom (see page 54) or Orange Cranberry Marmalade (see page 108).

4 tablespoons butter, melted

½ cup buckwheat flour

1 cup unbleached flour

2 teaspoons baking powder

1 teaspoon baking soda

½ teaspoon salt

1 cup buttermilk

4 large eggs

2 tablespoons maple syrup

Preheat the oven to 400°F. Butter a 12-muffin tin. Melt the butter and reserve.

Combine and blend together the buckwheat flour, unbleached flour, baking powder, baking soda, and salt in a mixing bowl. Make a well in the center. Pour the buttermilk, eggs, and maple syrup into the well. Mix the wet ingredients together with a fork. Gradually stir them into the dry ingredients with a spatula. When they are just mixed, fold in the melted butter.

Spoon the batter into the molds and bake for 15 minutes or until the muffins are puffed, browned, and register 200°F internally on an instant-read thermometer. Let them cool in the pan for 10 minutes. Unmold and serve muffins warm with butter and jam.

Grape-Nuts Muffins

In this recipe the rich wheat and malted barley aroma of Grape-Nuts is magnified by baking, and its famous gravel-crunch texture is softened to flavorful rubble. Try this muffin with the delicate Blueberry Jam with Mint (see page 56) or the sweet, hot Apple Ginger Jam (see page 29).

1 cup Grape-Nuts cereal

1 cup buttermilk

4 tablespoons unsalted butter, melted

4 eggs, lightly beaten

1 cup unbleached flour

2 teaspoons baking powder

1 teaspoon baking soda

2 tablespoons sugar

½ teaspoon salt

Preheat the oven to 400°F. Butter a 12-muffin tin.

Stir together the Grape-Nuts, buttermilk, melted butter, and eggs in a 1-quart bowl; let it stand for 10 minutes. Measure flour, baking powder, baking soda, sugar, and salt into a 2-quart bowl and stir well. Make a well in the dry ingredients and pour in the wet mixture. Stir the wet gradually into the dry until just blended.

Spoon the batter into the molds and bake for 15 minutes or until muffins are puffed, lightly browned, and register 200°F internally on an instant-read thermometer. Let them cool in the pan for 10 minutes. Unmold and serve muffins warm with sweet butter and jam.

Banana Bran Muffins

YIELD
12 MUFFINS

This muffin pairs soft, sweet bananas with the textured whole-grain flavors of wheat and bran. A colorful, acidic preserve such as Kiwifruit Pineapple Jam (see page 44) or Nectarine Orange Jam (see page 60) makes a tasty partner. You could also serve it with a zucchini or pepper marmalade and enjoy the combination of a vegetable preserve on dark bread.

- ⅔ cup wheat bran
- 1 cup whole-wheat flour
- ⅔ cup unbleached flour
- ¼ cup brown sugar
- ½ teaspoon salt
- 4 teaspoons baking powder
- 4 tablespoons unsalted butter, melted
- ½ cup milk
- 4 large eggs
- 2 large bananas, mashed (1 cup)

Preheat oven to 400°F. Butter a 12-muffin tin.

Combine the bran, flours, sugar, salt, and baking powder in a mixing bowl. Blend these ingredients together and make a well in the center. Stir melted butter, milk, and eggs together in a 2-cup measure. Pour the wet ingredients and the banana mash into the well of the dry mixture. Fold together until just blended.

Pour the batter into the mold and bake for 20 minutes or until the muffins are puffed, brown, and register 200°F internally on an instant-read thermometer. Let them cool in the pan for 5 minutes. Unmold and enjoy warm muffins with jam or marmalade.

Marmalade Muffins

YIELD
12 MUFFINS

- **2** cups unbleached flour
- **½** cup sugar
- **1** tablespoon baking powder
- **½** teaspoon sea salt
- **1** cup milk
- **6** tablespoons unsalted butter, melted
- **2** large eggs
- **1** teaspoon vanilla extract
- **¼** teaspoon almond extract
- **¼** cup orange marmalade
- **½** cup slivered almonds
- Confectioners' sugar

Preheat oven to 400°F. Butter a 12-muffin tin.

Combine and stir to blend the flour, sugar, baking powder, and salt in a large mixing bowl. Make a well in the center. Stir together the milk, butter, eggs, and extracts. Pour the liquid into the well, and stir together until just blended.

Fill the muffin molds half full with batter. Spoon a teaspoon of marmalade into the center of each mold. Top with the remaining batter. Scatter on the almond slivers.

Bake for 20 minutes or until the muffins are golden and register 200°F internally on an instant-read thermometer. Cool muffins on a rack for 10 minutes. Sprinkle on confectioners' sugar before serving.

Zucchini Bread

YIELD
1 LARGE LOAF OR 18 MUFFINS

This is one of my favorite summer breads. I never tire of making substitutions and variations in the recipe. But I always serve it the same way. Slices are cut thin. One side is slathered with fresh cream cheese, the other with Red Currant Jelly (see page 90) or an equally tangy Cherry Red Raspberry Jam (see page 34). The sandwiches are cut diagonally into triangles and served with a cup of hot tea.

2 cups grated zucchini

2 cups whole-wheat flour

1 cup unbleached white flour

1 cup sugar

1 teaspoon salt

1 teaspoon baking powder

1 teaspoon baking soda

¼ teaspoon each: mace, cinnamon, ginger, cardamom

3 large eggs

1 cup salad oil

2 teaspoons vanilla

Grated peel of 1 lemon (optional)

1 cup currants, chopped dried apricots and dates, or chopped nuts (optional)

Preheat oven to 325°F. Lightly oil a 9 × 5-inch loaf pan or an 18-muffin tin.

Grate the zucchini and reserve. Combine flours, sugar, salt, baking powder, baking soda, and spices in a 2-quart bowl, stir to mix, and make a well in the center. Add the eggs to the salad oil in a 2-cup measure and beat lightly. Stir in the vanilla.

Recipe continues on p. 170

Pour the wet ingredients into the well and stir from the center, slowly incorporating the dry into the wet ingredients. Mix only until a batter forms.

Fold in the zucchini along with optional lemon peel, dried fruits, or nuts, and pour the mixture into the pan or muffin tin.

Bake for 1 hour or until an instant thermometer inserted in the center of the loaf reaches 200°F. Allow the loaf to cool for 15 minutes in the pan (5 minutes for the muffins) before unmolding. Serve bread at room temperature (serve muffins warm) with an invigorating sweet-tart jelly.

Tea Brack

The tea in this recipe offers a slightly astringent counterpoint to the otherwise predominantly sweet ingredients. Tea Brack also has an attractively firm texture dotted with chewy sweet bits and crunchy nuts.

¾ cup white raisins

¾ cup dried currants

1¼ cups light brown sugar, firmly packed

1½ cups cold black tea

2 cups unbleached white flour

1½ teaspoons baking powder

½ teaspoon each: cinnamon and nutmeg

¼ teaspoon salt

½ cup walnuts, toasted and crushed

1 large egg

¼ cup salad oil

Combine raisins, currants, brown sugar, and tea in a mixing bowl. Cover and let stand overnight.

Preheat oven to 350°F and toast walnut halves for 10 minutes. Let the walnuts cool before crushing them to the size of peas. Turn the oven temperature down to 325°F. Generously oil a 9 × 5-inch loaf pan.

Blend flour, baking powder, spices, salt, and crushed walnuts in a large bowl. Make a well in the dry mixture. Add egg, oil, and tea mixture. Stir from the center, gradually adding the wet to the dry ingredients to make a smooth batter.

Pour batter into the prepared pan and bake for 1½ hours or until an instant thermometer inserted in the center of the loaf reaches 200°F.

Let the loaf cool in the pan for 30 minutes. Loosen the sides and invert to release the bread. Cool to room temperature before serving.

Cream Scones

This recipe produces a tender, buttery biscuit. Dress it with a truly fancy topping like Red Raspberry Preserves (see page 148). The preserves with liqueurs—Nectarine Jam with Grand Marnier (see page 46) and Pear Preserves with Pernod (see page 135)—make good partners as well.

2½ cups cake flour

¼ cup sugar

4 teaspoons baking powder

1 teaspoon salt

6 tablespoons cold unsalted butter

⅔ cup light cream

1 egg beaten with 1 tablespoon cream

Preheat oven to 375°F. Line a bake sheet with parchment.

Combine flour, sugar, baking powder, and salt in a 2-quart bowl and stir to mix. Cut the cold butter into 24 small pieces (quarter it lengthwise and cut each quarter crosswise into 6 pieces) and work it into the dry ingredients with fingertips or a pastry blender until the texture is mealy. Stir in cream until a ball forms. (If using a food processor, it will take 6 to 8 rapid on-and-off motions to pulverize the butter into the dry ingredients. Then add the cream and run the machine until a ball has barely formed.)

Roll the dough out ½ inch thick on a lightly floured work surface. Cut into 2½-inch biscuits with a cutter or the rim of a glass. Brush tops lightly with egg wash and bake for 15 minutes or until the scones are puffed and lightly browned. Cool them briefly and serve warm with jam or marmalade and Crème Fraîche (see page 218).

Buttermilk Currant Scones

YIELD: **18, 2-INCH SCONES**

SUBSTITUTE FOR LIGHT CREAM:

- **½** teaspoon baking soda
- **⅔** cup buttermilk

ADD:

- **½** cup currants

Follow directions for Cream Scones, above, with these modifications: Stir baking soda into buttermilk after butter is blended into dry ingredients. When buttermilk begins to foam, stir liquid into the dry ingredients to make a soft dough.

Fold in the currants on a lightly floured work surface, working the dough as little as possible. Proceed to roll out, cut, glaze, and bake the scones as indicated in the recipe above.

Drop Scones

YIELD
12 SCONES

The first scones were probably made as these are, dropped onto a hot griddle and baked quickly. They taste best split and eaten quite warm with butter and an intense flavor such as Apricot Orange Jam (see page 42) or Rhubarb Blackberry Jam (see page 40).

2	large eggs
5	tablespoons sugar
½	cup light cream
1½	cups cake flour
1	teaspoon baking powder

Preheat a griddle or heavy 12-inch skillet.

Beat the eggs and sugar together. Stir in the cream. Sift in the flour ½ cup at a time, adding the baking powder to the last addition, mixing each in thoroughly. (The scones will be the consistency of a thick pancake batter.)

Drop scones onto a hot griddle with a serving spoon (holds 2 tablespoons), and brown them on both sides for 5 to 6 minutes of total cooking time.

Serve hot immediately with marmalade and Crème Fraîche (see page 218).

Giant Sunday Popover

This giant popover's transformation from batter to a puffed and rippled, crispy brown pastry, trailing the scent of vanilla, is amazing to behold and will awaken an appetite in even the groggiest diner.

2 tablespoons salad oil

4 tablespoons unsalted butter

3 large eggs

¾ cup milk

¼ teaspoon vanilla extract

¼ teaspoon salt

½ tablespoon sugar

¾ cup unbleached flour, sifted before measuring

¼ teaspoon ground cinnamon

⅛ teaspoon ground ginger

¼ cup Vanilla Sugar (page 181)

1 cup Master Recipe for Fruit Sauce (page 213) made with Orange Cranberry Marmalade (page 108) or Apple Red Raspberry Preserves (page 151)

Preheat oven to 425°F. Combine oil and butter in an ovenproof 12-inch skillet. Put the skillet in the hot oven until butter begins to brown, 3 to 4 minutes.

Lightly beat the eggs with a whisk in a 2-quart bowl. Pour in the milk, vanilla, salt, and sugar, continuing to whisk gently. Sift the flour into a small bowl. Measure it, ¼ cup at a time, back into the sifter and onto the eggs and milk, whisking until each addition is just blended, though there may be small bits of unincorporated flour. Add the cinnamon and ginger to the last ¼ cup of flour.

Pour the batter into the hot skillet and return to oven to bake for 25 minutes. The popover will be puffed and brown. Dust the top with Vanilla Sugar and serve immediately in generous wedges. Pass warm Fruit Sauce at the table.

Apple Walnut Pancakes

YIELD

6 SERVINGS

²⁄₃ cup walnuts, toasted and chopped

2 cups all-purpose flour

¼ cup brown sugar

1 tablespoon baking powder

1 teaspoon salt

1 teaspoon cinnamon

½ teaspoon ground ginger

¼ teaspoon grated nutmeg

1⅓ cups milk

1⅓ cups apple purée (see Apple Jelly, page 92)

2 large eggs

2 tablespoons walnut, or vegetable, oil

Preheat the oven to 350°F. Toast the walnut halves on a baking sheet, cool, and chop.

Combine the dry ingredients: flour, brown sugar, baking powder, and seasonings in a mixing bowl and whisk together well. Make a well in the center. Combine the wet ingredients: milk, apple purée, eggs, and oil in a 1-quart measure and stir until well mixed. Pour the wet ingredients into the center of the dry mixture and blend until just mixed. Fold in the nuts.

Heat and lightly butter a large skillet. Ladle pancakes, using ⅓ of the batter, onto the skillet, leaving room for the pancakes to spread. Turn when bubbles appear in the cakes or after 2 minutes. Cook another 2 minutes. Serve immediately or hold in a preheated 300°F oven while making the remaining pancakes.

Serve with tart or intensely sweet and bitter preserves: Red Raspberry Preserves (see page 148) or Orange Marmalade (see pages 110, 111).

Apple Almond Waffles

2 cups all-purpose flour

¼ cup sugar

2 teaspoons baking powder

1 teaspoon baking soda

1 teaspoon sea salt

1 teaspoon allspice

1 cup buttermilk

1½ cups apple purée (see Apple Jelly, page 92)

2 large eggs

3 tablespoons butter, melted

⅔ cup toasted almonds, coarsely chopped

Preheat the waffle iron. Heat oven to 300°F.

Combine the dry ingredients: flour, sugar, baking powder, baking soda, salt, and allspice in a mixing bowl and whisk together well. Make a well in the center. Combine the wet ingredients: buttermilk, apple purée, eggs, and butter in a 1-quart measure and blend together well. Pour the wet ingredients into the center of the dry mixture and stir until just mixed. Fold in the nuts.

Lightly oil the hot waffle iron. Ladle a scant cup of batter over the surface of the iron and gently close it. When the light on the iron goes off, indicating the waffle is cooked, carefully lift the waffle onto a baking sheet and place it in the preheated oven to stay warm while continuing to make the remaining waffles, or serve immediately.

Russian Buckwheat Blinis with Blackberry Sauce

YIELD
12 BLINIS (4 SERVINGS)

This is a fitting breakfast for those who rise early to spend a day roving in the country or working in the yard. The ingredients have a wild, wayside appeal. The buckwheat blinis are griddlecakes with a yeasty and slightly bitter taste. The blackberries retain their woodsy floral scent and some acidity even when sweetened. Together they refresh and invigorate an awakening palate.

BLINIS

- **1** package dry active yeast (2¼ teaspoons)
- **½** cup lukewarm water
- **½** cup each: unbleached white flour and buckwheat flour
- **½** teaspoon salt
- **½** cup milk
- **2** large eggs, separated
- **1** stick (4 ounces) unsalted butter, melted

BLACKBERRY SAUCE

- **⅓** cup sugar
- **1** cup water
- **1** cup Rhubarb Blackberry Jam (page 40) or Strawberry Blackberry Jam (page 64)
  Freshly squeezed lemon juice

GARNISH

- **½** cup sour cream

BLINIS:

Add yeast and a pinch of sugar to the water. Wait 10 minutes for the yeast to dissolve and begin to foam. Combine flour and salt in a 2-quart mixing bowl and make a well in the center. Pour in milk, egg yolks, and yeast mixture. Stir wet into dry ingredients to make a smooth batter.

Cover the bowl with plastic wrap and let rise for 2 hours at room temperature or refrigerate overnight. If refrigerated, allow the risen batter to warm for an hour at room temperature. Warm the egg whites to room temperature.

Heat a 12-inch skillet or griddle and coat it lightly with butter. Beat egg whites to soft peaks. Spoon 2 tablespoons melted butter and ⅓ of egg whites onto the buckwheat batter and stir in gently. Fold in the remaining whites and butter in 2 installments.

Drop ⅓ cup batter at a time onto the hot skillet and cook until the underside is browned, 2 to 3 minutes. Turn the blinis and cook another minute or two. Slip browned blinis onto a warm plate and hold them in the oven at 300°F while preparing the rest.

BLACKBERRY SAUCE:

Make a simple syrup by combining the sugar and water in a saucepan and heating to a simmer. Cook the syrup for 5 minutes before stirring in the jam. Return mixture to a simmer. Season to taste with lemon juice.

GARNISH:

Serve blinis on warmed plates with Blackberry Sauce and a dab of sour cream.

French Toast with Plum Sauce

Day-old French bread is never discarded at our house. I turn it into an opportunity to enjoy French Toast, hot, puffed, and browned from the oven. We sprinkle each serving with Vanilla Sugar and pour on a sauce made from a fruit preserve with an assertive flavor and distinct fruit pieces, such as Plum Jam with Cardamom (see page 54), Spicy Cranberry Jam (see page 52), or Pear and Grape Preserves (see page 152).

FRENCH TOAST

4	large eggs
1	tablespoon sugar
½	teaspoon salt
¼	teaspoon each: ground cinnamon, nutmeg, ginger
¼	teaspoon vanilla extract
1	cup light cream
8–12	slices dry French bread (4–6 ounces)
3	tablespoons unsalted butter
2	tablespoons vegetable oil

VANILLA SUGAR

1	6-inch-long vanilla bean
1	cup granulated sugar

PLUM SAUCE

⅓	cup sugar
1	cup water
1	cup Plum Jam with Cardamom (page 54), Italian Plum Preserves (page 145), or Damson Plum Jam (page 53)
	Freshly squeezed lemon juice

Preheat oven to 425°F.

FRENCH TOAST:

Lightly beat eggs with a fork in a jelly roll pan. Stir in sugar, salt, spices, and vanilla. Slowly pour in the cream, stirring to mix well.

Add the bread slices to this custard mixture and let them soak for 3 minutes on each side or until slices are saturated but still hold their shape.

Combine butter and oil in a 12-inch ovenproof skillet or pan. Place it in the hot oven to heat the fats. Lay the soaked slices in the hot fats, return skillet to the oven, and bake for 7 minutes. Turn slices over and bake another 7 minutes.

VANILLA SUGAR:

Snip the vanilla bean into ¼-inch segments over the sugar. Pulverize this mixture in a food processor or blender. Sift out the pieces of vanilla bean. Stored in an airtight container, Vanilla Sugar will keep, becoming more fragrant, for several months.

PLUM SAUCE:

Make a simple syrup by combining the sugar and water in a saucepan and heating to a simmer. Cook the syrup for 5 minutes before stirring in the jam. Return the mixture to a simmer, and season to taste with lemon juice.

Serve the French Toast hot from the oven, lightly sprinkled with Vanilla Sugar. Pass the Plum Sauce at the table.

Risen Biscuits

The combination of yeast and baking powder gives these biscuits a high rise and a light texture. The biscuit is firm in the hand and crumbles easily in the mouth. A berry preserve adds just the right amount of texture in the mouth and a wild, woodsy scent to this eating experience. My favorites include Four-Berry Preserves (see page 146), Rhubarb Blackberry Jam (see page 40), and Blueberry Raspberry Preserves (see page 150).

If you make the variation of this recipe with fresh herbs, serve the biscuits with a wine or herb jelly.

1	package dry active yeast (2 ¼ teaspoons)
½	tablespoon sugar
¼	cup warm water (100°F)
2½	cups all-purpose flour
½	teaspoon salt
½	teaspoon baking powder
½	teaspoon baking soda
⅓	cup shortening
¾	cup buttermilk at room temperature
1	stick unsalted butter (4 ounces), melted

Add the yeast and sugar to the water. Wait 10 minutes for the yeast to dissolve and begin to foam. Combine the flour, salt, baking powder, and baking soda in a 4-quart mixing bowl. Cut in the shortening to make a fine, mealy texture with the dry ingredients. Pour on the foamy yeast and buttermilk and beat into a stiff dough. Turn the ball of dough out onto a lightly floured work surface and knead by hand 1 to 2 minutes, until it is taut and springy. Cover and let dough rest for 15 minutes. (If using a food processor, cut shortening into dry ingredients with rapid on-and-off motions. Add the buttermilk, then process until dough starts to ball. Knead by hand until taut and springy.)

Roll the dough out ½ inch thick and cut it into 2-inch rounds with a biscuit cutter.

Baste half the biscuit rounds with melted butter. Place the other biscuit rounds on top. Arrange biscuits 2 inches apart on a buttered and floured baking sheet. Cover them with plastic wrap and let rise in a warm, draft-free place for 1 hour.

Preheat oven to 375°F. Bake for 12 minutes or until richly browned and biscuits register 200°F degrees internally on an instant-read thermometer. Cool the biscuits briefly on a wire rack and serve warm.

VARIATION

Risen Herb Twist Biscuits

YIELD: 14 BISCUITS

Biscuit Dough (preceding recipe)

1 large egg yolk beaten with 1 tablespoon water

½ cup minced fresh herbs (parsley, chives, dill, rosemary)

½ teaspoon dried thyme, powdered

½ teaspoon powdered ginger

Prepare the biscuit dough using preceding recipe, excluding the butter. Roll the biscuit dough into an 8 × 12-inch rectangle on a lightly floured sheet of parchment paper. Brush the beaten egg yolk over the entire surface and sprinkle on the herbs and ginger. Roll up the dough along its wider side, brushing more yolk mixture on the exposed underside of the dough as it is rolled up.

Tightly pinch the edge closed. Slice the biscuit roll into 14 pieces with a sharp knife. Space the rolls 2 inches apart on a prepared baking sheet, cover with plastic wrap, and let them rise in a warm, draft-free place for 1 hour.

Brush the biscuits with the remaining egg yolk mixture and bake as directed in the Risen Biscuits recipe above.

Spiced Applesauce Cake

CAKE BATTER

¾	cup Granny Smith apple puree
½	cup water
2	teaspoons vanilla extract or paste
1	tablespoon apple cider vinegar
1½	cups unbleached white flour
⅓	cup sugar
¾	teaspoon salt
¾	teaspoon baking powder
¼	teaspoon cinnamon
¼	teaspoon powdered star anise or ginger

FROSTING

4	ounces cream cheese at room temperature
2	tablespoons unsalted butter at room temperature
½	teaspoon orange extract
¼	teaspoon sea salt
9	ounces powdered sugar, sifted

CAKE:

Preheat the oven to 350°F. Oil an 8-inch square baking pan. Line it with parchment paper and oil the paper.

Whisk the wet ingredients together. Stir the dry ingredients together in a separate bowl. Fold the dry ingredients into the wet ones in 3 installments until just mixed. Pour the batter into the prepared mold and smooth the surface with a spatula. Bake for 20 minutes. Top will be firm and internal temperature will reach 200°F. Cool on a rack before frosting.

FROSTING:

Break up the cream cheese into small chunks. Combine it with the butter in an electric stand or hand mixer. Blend the ingredients together on a low speed. Add the extract and salt. Work in the sugar, ½ cup at a time until smooth.

English Muffins

Homemade English Muffins, eaten warm, are simply light years away from the dry sponges that pose as muffins in the supermarket. They are so simple to assemble, it's a wonder homemade muffins aren't the norm. Of all the breads tested for this book, this was my family's favorite.

It's their yeasty aroma and chewy texture that make English Muffins unique. I serve them with any of the preserves that have texture and tangy flavor.

1   package dry active yeast (2 ¼ teaspoons)

¾   cup water at room temperature, divided

1   cup milk, warmed to 70°F

4   cups unbleached white flour

1   teaspoon salt

Stir the yeast into ½ cup water and leave it to dissolve and foam for 5 to 10 minutes. Add the milk and reserve. Combine the flour and salt in the work bowl of a mixer or large mixing bowl. Pour the milk mixture into the dry ingredients with the machine running. Beat at medium speed with a paddle attachment or by hand as a dough forms. Watch to see that the dough sticks equally to the beaters or handheld spatula and the sides of the bowl. If the dough is stiff, add as much of the remaining ¼ cup water as needed to create this consistency. Beat for 3 minutes by hand or in an electric mixer until the dough is quite elastic.

Let the dough rise, covered, in a protected place at about 75°F until it doubles in size. This will take about 1 hour.

Heat a cast-iron griddle or heavy aluminum 12-inch skillet. Oil the interior of several muffin rings and fit them into the skillet. (You can make your own rings from pet food tins by removing the tops and bottoms.)

Punch down the risen dough and tear off a ⅓-cup piece. It will be sticky and stretchable. Place it in a muffin ring on the hot surface. Fill remaining rings the same way.

Bake muffins 10 minutes on each side and continue turning at 5-minute intervals until an instant-read thermometer inserted through the center of the muffin registers 200°F. Release the muffins from the rings, re-oil, and continue with remaining dough. Let muffins cool for 15 minutes on a wire rack, pull them apart with fingers, fork, or special muffin opener, and serve warm with sweet butter and preserves.

VARIATIONS

Whole-Wheat English Muffins

Substitute 1 cup whole-wheat flour for 1 cup of the unbleached white flour in the master recipe above. Follow the same directions as for the master recipe.

Buckwheat English Muffins

Substitute ½ cup each of buckwheat and whole-wheat flour for 1 cup of the unbleached white flour in the master recipe above. Follow the same directions as for the master recipe.

English Muffins with Yogurt

One way to flatter a sweet preserve is to serve it with a slightly tart bread. Instead of making a sourdough bread, which is more time-consuming, I added feta cheese and yogurt to the easy English Muffin recipe. When you eat this yogurt muffin along with sweet butter, savor the added dimension its lightly sour element brings to this yeasty, chewy bread. Serve it with Strawberry Preserves (see page 141) or Italian Plum Preserves (see page 145).

Recipe continues on p. 188

  1 package dry active yeast (2¼ teaspoons)
  1 cup water at room temperature, divided
1½ cups bread flour
1½ cups unbleached white flour
  2 teaspoons salt
  4 ounces feta cheese, grated
  1 cup plain yogurt, at room temperature

Stir the yeast into ½ cup water and leave it to dissolve and foam for 5 to 10 minutes. Combine the flours and salt in a 3-quart bowl. Make a well in the center of the dry ingredients and add grated cheese, yeast mixture, and yogurt. Stir these wet ingredients into the dry to make a thick batter. When stirred, the dough will stick in equal parts to the stirring tool and the sides of the bowl. If the dough is stiff, add as much of the remaining ¼ cup water as needed to create this consistency. Beat by hand or in an electric mixer for 3 minutes, until the dough is quite elastic.

Let the batter rise, covered, in a protected place at about 75°F until it doubles in size. This will take about 1 hour.

Follow cooking directions given in master recipe above.

CHAPTER

9

Desserts

HOMEMADE FRUIT PRESERVES ARE TOO TASTY to be limited to breakfast or tea. They offer a head start, an inspiration really, for any number of dessert preparations. In this chapter, we begin with fruit sauces, the easiest possible use. After you thin a jam with Simple Syrup (see page 212), it is ready-made as a topping for fruit, ice cream, or cake. I've provided some combinations to get you started.

A fruit preserve doesn't have to sit on a plate either. If you offer an English gentleman of a certain age a goblet filled with preserves loosely folded into whipped cream, he'll thank you for remembering his fondness for an old-fashioned Fruit Fool, like the ones his mother used to make. The French slather sweet crêpes with jam to eat on the street or flame them with cognac for a dressy dessert presentation. On this side of the Atlantic, a rich Blueberry Sauce enlivens the classic American cheesecake.

It may come as a surprise to learn that fruit preserves can also be transformed into ingenious fountain treats. They offer an inviting texture and concentrated flavor when frozen. Take your pick between a fruit sorbet made by freezing a preserve that has been thinned with sugar syrup or an ice cream created with the addition of light cream or egg custard to a jam or preserve. The master recipes in this chapter have freezing directions for those with and those without an ice cream machine.

Traditional British sweets inspired me to include recipes that layer fruit preserves in bread puddings and a showy fruit trifle. These desserts involve combining simple recipes to make an impressive dessert for a special occasion. If your preference is for lighter fare, try the Souffléd Pudding made with marmalade (see page 197). I don't know which is more impressive, its magical rise in the oven or the length of time it stays puffed after you've removed it.

Legend has it that British housewives are fiercely proud of their fruit preserves and love to showcase their preserving prowess by filling a single pastry shell with as many as seven jams covered with a lattice crust. I chose to include an Austrian Linzer Torte (see page 208), filled with rich raspberry preserves.

Fresh Pears with Blackberry Sauce

YIELD
6 SERVINGS

This is a wonderful last-minute dessert for family and guests. If you have time to prepare the pears an hour or two before dinner, the syrup will protect their color and freshness in the refrigerator. The sauce is so easy that it invites improvisation with an infusion of lemon verbena or mint.

- **6** firm, ripe Bartlett pears
- **2** cups Simple Syrup (page 212)
- **⅔** cup Blackberry Ginger Preserves (page 147), No-Sugar Apple Blackberry Jam (page 72), or Blueberry Blackberry Preserves (page 140)
- **2** tablespoons blackberry brandy or 1 teaspoon fresh lemon juice

Peel and halve the pears. Remove stems and blossom ends with a paring knife. Scoop out cores with the small cup of a melon-baller. Lay pear halves in a shallow bowl filled with Simple Syrup. Coat them well and chill. (This may be done 2 to 3 hours in advance but not the night before.)

When ready to serve, combine the preserves with ⅓ cup of the syrup covering the pears in a small skillet. Warm over low heat and stir to make a smooth sauce. Add the brandy or lemon juice and simmer 30 seconds. Drain the pears and divide them among 6 dessert bowls. Spoon the warm fruit sauce over the pears and serve immediately.

Baked Peach Halves with Blueberry Sauce

YIELD
6 SERVINGS

2 tablespoons chopped toasted pecans

6 ripe Freestone peaches

⅓ cup crumbled macaroon cookies

¼ cup fresh blueberries

3 tablespoons crème de cassis, divided

SAUCE

½ cup Spicy Blueberry Preserves (page 138) or Blueberry Jam with Mint (page 56)

2 tablespoons Simple Syrup (page 212)

1 tablespoon fresh lemon juice

1 tablespoon crème de cassis (optional)

Preheat oven to 350°F. Toast the pecan halves on a baking sheet in the oven for 10 minutes. Cool on the baking sheet, coarsely chop, and reserve. Generously butter a large, shallow baking dish.

Halve the peaches, remove the pits, and enlarge the hollows in each half by scooping out 1 teaspoon of flesh with a melon-baller or grapefruit spoon. Crush together these small peach pieces with the macaroons, add the warm pecans, blueberries, and 2 tablespoons of cassis. Fill the craters of each peach half with this stuffing.

Arrange peaches in the buttered baking dish so they are not touching. Baste each lightly with cassis and bake for 30 minutes. Remove peaches from the oven and let them cool in the pan.

SAUCE:

Warm the preserves with the syrup in a small saucepan. Add the lemon juice and optional cassis. Serve the peaches at room temperature or chilled with the warm sauce.

Fresh Peach Melba

YIELD
6 SERVINGS

This is the perfect dessert to eat when the weather is hot and you have an excess of super-ripe peaches. The combination of flavors and temperatures is incomparable: cold, rich ice cream; sweet, fresh peaches; and warm, tart raspberries. It's a dessert I long for during the winter months.

1 cup Red Raspberry Preserves (pages 133, 148)

⅓ cup Simple Syrup (page 212)

1–2 tablespoons raspberry brandy (optional)

6 ripe Freestone peaches

1 pint vanilla ice cream

Heat preserves and syrup to a simmer in a skillet, stirring until smooth. Add brandy if desired. Allow the sauce to cool slightly.

Dip the peaches in boiling water for 30 seconds. Cool under running water, peel, halve to remove the stones, and thinly slice. Divide peach slices among 6 glass serving bowls or goblets. Place a generous scoop of ice cream on the fruit. Top each serving with 3 tablespoons warm raspberry sauce. Serve immediately.

Master Recipe for Fruit Sorbets

A homemade jam diluted with Simple Syrup and frozen becomes a silken sorbet worthy of a special occasion or summer party. There's no need for an ice cream freezer, either. This thinned preserve can be poured onto a baking sheet, left in the freezer compartment, and just 2 hours later scooped out soft-frozen into serving goblets. The concentrated nature of the preserves guarantees a supple, stick-to-the-tongue succulence. These sorbets also retain their shape well and do not separate in storage.

2 cups fruit jam, no-sugar jam, or berry preserve

2 cups Simple Syrup (page 212)

1 tablespoon (or more) fresh lemon or lime juice

Combine a jam or preserve with an equal volume of syrup. Stir them together. Add lemon or lime juice to balance the sweetness with a bit of tartness.

FREEZING WITHOUT AN ICE CREAM FREEZER

Freeze sorbet on a shallow baking sheet at 0°F. It will be soft-frozen within 2 hours. Spoon into goblets or sherbet glasses and serve immediately.

FREEZING WITH AN ICE CREAM FREEZER

Chill the sorbet. Stir it well and pour into an ice cream machine. Freeze it, following the instructions that come with the machine.

Master Recipe for Philadelphia-Style Ice Cream

1 QUART

This simple combination yields a light, fruit-forward ice cream. Preserves with a loose texture and assertive fruit flavor such as Nectarine Jam with Grand Marnier (see page 46), Seedless Black Raspberry Jam (see page 38), or Strawberry Blackberry Preserves (see page 144) are ideal choices for this ice cream. If you don't consume it all the first day, keep it in the freezer until the next time you serve it, and its creamy texture will return as it softens.

2 cups half-and-half (light cream)

1½ cups fruit jam or preserves

Stir half-and-half into jam or preserves.

FREEZING WITHOUT AN ICE CREAM FREEZER

Still-freeze on a shallow pan, tightly covered. Break up the semi-frozen cream with a fork after the first hour, and twice more at ½-hour intervals.

FREEZING WITH AN ICE CREAM FREEZER

Chill this mixture for 1 hour. Stir and freeze according to the instructions that accompany your ice cream freezer. Allow the soft-frozen ice cream to ripen in the freezer for 2 to 4 hours before serving.

Master Recipe for Preserves in Ice Cream Custard

YIELD
3½ CUPS

Pair this recipe's creamy, yolk-enriched custard base with one of the more intense and luxurious fruit flavors, such as Four-Berry Preserves (see page 146), Peach Preserves with Raspberries (see page 142), or Blueberry Jam with Mint (see page 56).

- **1** cup half-and-half (light cream)
- **1** cup whipping cream
- **3** large egg yolks
- **1⅓** cups jam or preserves

Combine the half-and-half with the whipping cream in a heavy, non-reactive pan and heat to scalding (180°F).

Beat the yolks lightly in a small bowl. Gradually pour in 1 cup hot cream mixture, stirring constantly. Return the yolk-enriched cream to the pan and cook briefly over low heat until the custard coats the spoon (166°F). Sieve the custard into a bowl. Stir preserves into the hot liquid, and mix until it reaches a smooth consistency.

Refrigerate this base until it is thoroughly chilled, 2 to 4 hours. Freeze according to instructions below.

FREEZING WITHOUT AN ICE CREAM FREEZER

Still-freeze on a shallow pan, tightly covered. Break up the semi-frozen cream with a fork after the first hour, and twice more at ½-hour intervals.

FREEZING WITH AN ICE CREAM FREEZER

Stir and freeze according to the instructions that accompany your ice cream freezer. Allow the soft-frozen ice cream to ripen in the freezer for 2 to 4 hours before serving.

Lemon Amaretto Souffléed Pudding with Raspberry Sauce

The ethereal appearance and texture of this soufflé are deceptive. Without an extra egg white, common to soufflés, this pudding is quite sturdy. It emerges from its hot water bath fully puffed, with the staying power and rich flavor of a pudding.

SOUFFLÉ

- **⅔** cup Lemon Ginger Marmalade (page 116)
- **⅔** cup Simple Syrup (page 212)
- **3** tablespoons Amaretto
- **2** tablespoons cornstarch
- **4** large eggs, separated, room temperature
- **3** tablespoons sugar

RASPBERRY SAUCE

- **1** cup Red Raspberry Preserves (pages 133, 148)
- **½** cup Simple Syrup (page 212)
- **1½** tablespoons crème de cassis liqueur, optional
- **1** teaspoon strained fresh lemon juice
- **12** perfect red raspberries

SOUFFLÉ:

Generously butter and sugar a 6-cup soufflé mold. Refrigerate it. Preheat the oven to 325°F.

Mix the Lemon Ginger Marmalade and syrup in a small saucepan. Dissolve the cornstarch in the Amaretto and stir into the pan. Heat this base, stirring constantly, until it reaches a simmer and thickens noticeably.

Recipe continues on p. 198

Turn the hot marmalade mixture into a 2-quart bowl. Stir in the egg yolks, one at a time.

Beat egg whites with 2 tablespoons sugar to soft peaks. Add remaining sugar to make a firm meringue. Stir ⅓ of the whites into the marmalade mixture. Fold in remaining whites in two parts.

To fold, use a circular motion with a rubber spatula straight down into the center of the whites, flat along the bottom, and up the side, lifting whites to cover the ingredients on the surface before returning to the center again. Turn this circle into a doughnut shape by turning the bowl and repeating this action until only streaks of the ingredient being added still show.

Gently spoon the mixture into the chilled mold. Place mold in a pan of boiling water to half the height of the mold and bake for 40 minutes. (Soufflé may be held in the refrigerator for 30 minutes before baking.)

SAUCE:

Warm the preserves with simple syrup and strain to remove seeds. Stir in the optional liqueur and lemon juice. Refrigerate until serving time.

Serve soufflé hot at the table. Surround each serving with cool raspberry sauce and a few fresh berries.

VARIATION

Orange Marmalade Souffléed Pudding with Grand Marnier Sauce

For the soufflé, substitute ⅔ cup Orange Marmalade II (see page 111) for Lemon Ginger Marmalade. Stir the cornstarch into Grand Marnier instead of Amaretto, and proceed as described above.

For the sauce, stir 2 tablespoons Grand Marnier into ¼ cup Crème Fraîche (see page 218), and spoon a dollop onto each serving.

Master Recipe for Crêpes

YIELD
12 CRÊPES (6 SERVINGS)

2 large eggs

1 cup milk

⅓ cup water

1 cup all-purpose flour

2 tablespoons sugar

1 teaspoon vanilla extract

¼ teaspoon sea salt

3 tablespoons melted butter, divided

In the work bowl of a food processor or blender, combine the eggs, milk, water, flour, sugar, vanilla, salt, and 2 tablespoons melted butter. Run the machine for 5 seconds or until mixture is smooth. Scrape down the sides of the bowl and process briefly again. This batter may be used right away or refrigerated up to 24 hours. Before using, stir briefly to blend ingredients.

Heat a 6-inch non-stick crêpe pan or shallow skillet. Brush on a bit of the remaining tablespoon of butter. Pour in 3 tablespoons of batter (a scant ¼ cup) and immediately tilt the pan to allow the batter to coat the entire surface. Let the batter cook for 1 to 2 minutes until the batter looks dry on the surface and the edge is crisp. Loosen the edge of the crêpe with a spatula and slide a wooden crepe paddle or spatula 4 inches under the crêpe, lift, and turn it over in the pan. After 30 seconds, lift the crepe out or turn over the pan and drop it on a wax paper-lined plate. Repeat with remaining batter, stacking the completed crêpes on the plate.

Crêpes may be held at room temperature, plastic-wrapped, for 2 to 3 hours, refrigerated for 3 to 5 days, or frozen.

Berry Jam Crêpes Flambées

CRÊPES

1 Master Recipe for Crêpes (page 199)

¾ cup berry jam, any kind

SYRUP AND ASSEMBLY

1 cup water

½ cup sugar

4 tablespoons cognac or berry-flavored liqueur

1 cup mixed berries

GARNISH

1 cup lightly whipped cream

CRÊPES:

Prepare crêpes as instructed in Master Recipe. Spread 1 to 2 tablespoons of berry jam (any kind) over each crêpe. Fold the crêpe into quarters so it resembles a pie-shaped wedge. Repeat with remaining crêpes.

SYRUP AND ASSEMBLY:

Combine water and sugar in a large skillet and bring to a simmer, stirring to dissolve the sugar. Cook for 1 minute.

Place the crêpe wedges in the warm syrup over low heat. Turn them in the syrup to coat. Pour on the cognac (or berry-flavored liqueur) and ignite immediately. When flames have died down, divide the crêpes among 6 plates. Add the berries to the skillet and shake the pan to coat them with syrup.

GARNISH:

Spoon berries, with syrup, onto each serving and add a dollop of whipped cream.

Bread and Jam Pudding

YIELD
8–10 SERVINGS

2 large eggs

2 large egg yolks

1 tablespoon sugar

½ teaspoon vanilla extract

¼ teaspoon salt

1½ cups half-and-half (light cream)

1½ cups milk

18–24 slices day-old French bread (10–12 ounces)

1¼ cups jam such as Rhubarb Blackberry (page 40), Cherry Red Raspberry (page 34), Seedless Black Raspberry (page 38), or Strawberry Rhubarb (page 27)

Garnish with Crème Fraîche (page 218) and fresh berries or fruit slices to match the preserves (optional)

Preheat the oven to 350°F. Generously butter an 8 × 12-inch gratin dish.

Whisk together the eggs and yolks, then whisk in the sugar, vanilla, and salt. Stir in the cream and milk.

Place half the bread slices at the bottom of the gratin dish. Trim pieces to fill in spaces between slices, as needed. Cover the slices with half the custard. Let the bread absorb the custard for a few minutes, then generously spread the bread with jam. Repeat with the second layer.

Allow the pudding to sit for 10 minutes to completely absorb the custard. Cover the dish with foil buttered on the side facing the pudding. Bake for 30 minutes. Remove and turn the oven heat up to 375°F. Remove the foil and bake another 10 minutes.

Let the pudding cool to warm before serving. Accompany with Crème Fraîche and fresh fruit or berry pieces, if desired.

Orange Bread Pudding

The idea of a dessert combining sweet, sour, and bitter flavors in a creamy pudding was inspired by a most satisfying cabinet pudding I was served at the Jovan restaurant in Chicago thirty years ago. A dark stratum of rye bread woven into the white added sour overtones to the creamy, custard-saturated loaf. The pudding floated in a lightly bitter caramel and sherry sauce studded with raisins.

1 recipe English Custard (page 215) made with ¼ cup Grand Marnier

12 ounces day-old white sandwich bread, crusts trimmed

8 ounces day-old seedless rye bread, crusts trimmed, cut into ½-inch cubes

1½ cups Orange Marmalade (pages 110, 111)

½ cup sherry, divided

Garnish with 1 cup whipped cream or Crème Fraîche (page 218) and fresh orange sections

Preheat the oven to 350°F. Generously butter an 8 × 12-inch gratin dish.

Make the custard, adding the Grand Marnier in place of the vanilla.

Place a bread layer in the dish using ⅓ of the sandwich bread slices. Pour on ⅓ of the custard and wait a few minutes for the bread to absorb it. Spread ¾ cup of the marmalade over the bread. Scatter half the rye cubes over this layer and sprinkle it with ¼ cup sherry. Lay another ⅓ of the sandwich bread slices, pour on another ⅓ of the custard, wait until it is absorbed, and spread on the remaining marmalade. Repeat once more with the remaining rye cubes, ¼ cup sherry, and remaining bread slices, finishing with custard.

Allow the dish to sit for 10 minutes to allow the bread to absorb the custard. Bake, covered with buttered foil, for 30 minutes in the upper half of the oven. Remove from the oven and uncover. Return the dish to the oven and turn up the heat to 375°F. Bake another 10 minutes. Let the pudding cool to warm before serving. Serve with whipped cream or Crème Fraîche and fresh orange sections, if desired.

Rhubarb Ginger Fool

YIELD
8-12 SERVINGS

The English gave the name fruit fool to a light bit of fruity dessert at the end of a meal. It's rich with heavy cream and tart with rhubarb, a replacement for the hard-to-find gooseberry used in the original. A fruit fool is an easy way to surprise your guests with a festive and refreshing finale to a spring or summer meal.

- **1** cup Rhubarb Ginger Jam (page 39)
- **⅓** cup Simple Syrup (page 212)
  Fresh lemon juice
- **1½** cups whipping cream
- **2** tablespoons crystallized ginger, cut into thin strips

Combine the jam, syrup, and just enough lemon juice to accent sweet and spicy flavors.

Beat the cream to soft peaks and spoon it into a 1-quart decorative glass bowl. Fold the jam mixture into the cream, leaving streaks of pink to alternate with white. (To fold, make a circular motion with a rubber spatula straight down into the center of the whipping cream, proceed flat along the bottom, and then go up the sides, lifting whites to cover the jam. Turn this circle into a doughnut shape by repeating this action while turning the bowl until the ingredients are mixed.)

This recipe can be made 2 to 3 hours ahead and held refrigerated in a serving bowl or in individual goblets. Scatter on ginger strips at serving time.

Jam Tart

YIELD
6 SERVINGS

A tart filled with one of your own preserves and garnished with fresh fruit offers an unusually tasty and light pastry. If the preserver's well-stocked larder includes a home-made jelly with which to glaze the fresh tart, the effect is professional. A sprinkling of confectioners' sugar will work as a finishing touch as well.

1 pre-baked 11-inch Tart Shell Pastry (page 214)

1½ cups (12 ounces) jam, preserves, or marmalade (see list below)

Whole fruit, thinly sliced, or 1 pint berries (see list below)

⅓ cup melted Red Currant Jelly (page 90) or Cinnamon Cranberry Apple Jelly (page 88) for glaze or confectioners' sugar

Spread the preserves in an even layer on the pre-baked tart shell in a springform pan. Prepare fruit that is complementary to the filling: peel, core, and thinly slice apples; peel and cut segments from oranges or grapefruits; cut other fruits or berries into bite-sized pieces. Spread slices in a layered wreath over the preserves. Dot whole berries over the top.

Brush the fruit with melted jelly or dust with confectioners' sugar.

SUGGESTED FLAVOR COMBINATIONS

- Apple Red Raspberry Preserves with thin apple slices and fresh raspberries. Glaze with Cinnamon Cranberry Apple Jelly.

- Apple Grape Preserves with apple slices and Cinnamon Cranberry Apple Jelly glaze.

- Any of the berry preserves or jams with fresh berries and Red Currant Jelly glaze.

- Kiwifruit Mint Jam with kiwifruit and strawberry slices and Cinnamon Cranberry Apple Jelly.

- Raspberry Pear Jam with pear slices and Cinnamon Cranberry Apple Jelly.

- Orange Marmalade with orange segments and strained marmalade glaze instead of jelly.

- Orange Cranberry Marmalade with orange segments and Cinnamon Cranberry Apple Jelly.

- Grapefruit Marmalade with grapefruit segments and strained marmalade glaze instead of jelly.

Blueberry Pecan Cheesecake

YIELD
16–20 SERVINGS

Homemade preserves and textured jams make delicious garnishes for cheesecake. This recipe is my standby cake, and it can serve as a model for any number of your own improvisations.

CRUST

- **½** cup pecan halves
- **10** ounces pecan sandie cookies
- **4** tablespoons unsalted butter, melted

FILLING

- **1** cup sugar
- **1** teaspoon salt
- **3** tablespoons flour
- **2** pounds cream cheese or Neufchâtel
- **1½** teaspoons vanilla extract
- **3** large eggs
- **2** cups sour cream

TOPPING

- **1½** cups (12 ounces) Spicy Blueberry Preserves (page 138), Blueberry Jam with Mint (page 56), or Blueberry Blackberry Preserves (page 140)

Preheat oven to 350°F. Toast the pecan halves on a bake sheet for 10 minutes. Cool.

CRUST:

Reduce the cookies and pecans to fine crumbs in a food processor or blender with rapid on-and-off motions. Sprinkle on the butter and process for 5 seconds. Press crust mixture into the bottom and two-thirds of the way up the sides of a 9-inch springform pan. Refrigerate the pan while assembling the filling.

FILLING:

Measure sugar, salt, and flour into a 1-quart bowl. Stir ingredients together until they are well blended. Place cream cheese in a mixing bowl or work bowl of either an electric mixer or food processor. Process the cheese until smooth. Mix in the vanilla and the eggs, one at a time, stirring to keep mixture smoothly blended. Work in the sour cream one cup at a time.

Add dry ingredients to the filling and stir for 1 minute by hand, 30 seconds in a mixer, or 15 seconds in a food processor. Scrape down the sides of the bowl. Pour the filling into the chilled crust and bake for 50 minutes. The cake's top should be puffed, firm, and lightly browned.

Cool the cake on a wire rack for 30 minutes. Run a knife along the inside of the collar before releasing and removing it. Refrigerate the cake once it has come to room temperature.

TOPPING:

Thirty minutes before serving time, spread the preserves over the top of the cake. Return to chill until serving.

CHEESECAKE VARIATIONS

Use the same cake filling as in the preceding recipe but substitute a different cookie for the crust (omit the pecan halves). Select a preserve topping that flatters this new cake and crust combination. Try the combinations below or invent your own.

Any of the ginger-spiced jams, such as Rhubarb Ginger Jam (see page 39) or Blackberry Ginger Preserves (see page 147), would be terrific with a gingersnap cookie crust.

Cherry Vanilla Jam (see page 35), with its pure vanilla accent, would taste great in tandem with a rich vanilla wafers crust.

Linzer Torte

YIELD
10–12 SERVINGS

This famous Austrian pastry is a great way to showcase any of your homemade pre-serves, especially those with raspberries. To heighten the fresh raspberry flavor, I have substituted hazelnuts for almonds, usually added to the crust. These nuts, known as filberts in the U. S., have a sweetness that pairs beautifully with the tart raspberries.

PASTRY

1	cup raw hazelnuts (5 ounces)
1½	cups unbleached flour
⅛	teaspoon cloves
¼	teaspoon cinnamon
⅓	cup sugar
	Grated zest of 1 lemon
1	cup unsalted butter (2 sticks)
2	ounces cream cheese
2	large egg yolks
½	tablespoon vanilla extract

FILLING

1½	cups Red Raspberry Preserves (pages 133, 148), Four-Berry Preserves (page 146), or Cherry Red Raspberry Jam (page 34)

GLAZE

1	large egg yolk
2	teaspoons cream

GARNISH

¼	cup confectioners' sugar

Preheat oven to 350°F. Toast the hazelnuts in the oven for 10 minutes. Rub the warm nuts in a tea towel to remove their brown skins. Butter the bottom and sides of a 9-inch springform pan. Line the pan with parchment paper and butter the paper.

PASTRY ASSEMBLY BY HAND:

Crush the nuts in a mortar and pestle. Blend with the flour, spices, sugar, and lemon zest. Allow the butter and cream cheese to come to room temperature. Cream them with egg yolks and vanilla, then work in the dry ingredient mixture.

PASTRY ASSEMBLY IN A FOOD PROCESSOR:

Pulverize the nuts with the other dry ingredients, using rapid on-and-off pulses in a processor. Quarter the sticks of butter lengthwise and cut each stick into 8 pieces across. Cut the cream cheese into teaspoon-sized bits. Blend these cold ingredients, along with the egg yolks and vanilla, into the dry ingredients until a dough begins to form.

Shape the dough into a flat disk, lightly flour it, wrap it airtight in plastic, and chill for 1 hour. Remove the dough from the refrigerator. Cut off ⅓ of the dough, wrap it, and return it to the refrigerator. Roll the larger piece of dough between layers of plastic wrap into a circle 1 inch larger than the diameter of the pan. Remove the top layer of plastic and turn the dough into the pan, remove the plastic wrap, and press the dough evenly onto the bottom and up the sides of the pan.

FILLING:

Spread the preserves evenly on the dough. Remove the remaining piece of dough from the refrigerator and roll it about ¼ inch thick on a lightly floured surface. Cut ½-inch-wide strips and lay half of them parallel to one another at 1-inch intervals over the preserves. Turn the pan 90 degrees and repeat the parallel strips to form a lattice. Press the ends of the strips into the dough where they meet the the rim of the shell and trim off the excess. Use a paring knife to fold the dough above the preserves to make a thick border around the edge of the pan, sealing and framing the lattice.

Recipe continues on p. 210

GLAZE:

Beat together the egg yolk and cream. Baste all pastry surfaces with this glaze and refrigerate the torte for ½ hour.

Bake for 45 minutes or until the torte is richly browned. Let it cool 10 minutes before removing the springform sides. Slide the torte off the pan bottom onto a serving tray when it has come to room temperature.

GARNISH:

Dust the top with confectioners' sugar.

Strawberry Trifle

Surprise your dinner guests by first announcing you have "just a trifle" for dessert. Then bring in this stunning creation of jam-spiraled sponge cake filled with a rich vanilla custard and topped with whipped cream. Don't you love the English knack for understatement?

1   sheet Jelly Roll Sponge Cake (page 216)

½   cup medium-sweet sherry, divided

1½   cups Strawberry Preserves (page 132, 141)

1½   recipes of English Custard (page 215)

1   cup whipped cream

Remove the waxed paper protecting the top surface of the cake. Trim crusty edges and sprinkle the cake with 2 tablespoons of sherry.

Spread on the Strawberry Preserves and use a long sheet of waxed paper under the cake to help roll up the cake along the long edge. Cut the jelly roll cake into 18 slices.

Lay the jelly roll slices side-by-side on the bottom and up the sides of a 2-quart glass serving bowl, reserving 6 slices for the top. Sprinkle the remaining sherry over the cake slices. Pour on the English Custard. Make a layer of jelly roll slices on top of the custard. Cover and chill at least 2 hours before serving. (It can be held for several hours or overnight.)

At serving time, with a rosette-tipped pipe, form a decorative pattern over the top of the trifle with whipped cream. You can also spoon out the trifle and add a dollop of whipped cream to each plate as it is served.

Simple Syrup

Simple Syrup is the cooked sugar and water medium that makes preserve-based sauces and frozen sorbets possible. The added tablespoon of lemon juice in the syrup plays a dual role as catalyst to dissolve the sugar and to balance the flavor.

3 cups water

1 cup granulated sugar

1 tablespoon strained fresh lemon juice

Combine water, sugar, and lemon juice in a heavy, non-reactive 2-quart saucepan. Heat, stirring occasionally, until the sugar dissolves. Let the syrup cool to room temperature and transfer it to a storage jar. It will keep, refrigerated, for as long as 2 months.

Master Recipe for Fruit Sauce Made from Jams and Preserves

YIELD
2 CUPS

Although proportions are specified in this recipe, you may use them with flexibility, thinning fruit preserves to the consistency you desire for each dessert. Add lemon juice one teaspoon at a time, tasting after each addition, until you reach a balance of sweet and sour elements.

1½ cups fruit jam or preserves

½ cup (or more) Simple Syrup (page 212)

Fresh lemon juice, to taste

Heat jam or preserves with ½ cup Simple Syrup in a heavy, non-reactive 1-quart saucepan, stirring constantly until the jam has thoroughly liquified into a sauce. Thin with additional syrup if the sauce is too thick to coat a spoon lightly and evenly. Off the heat, add lemon juice by the teaspoon, tasting after each addition, to balance the sweetness of the sauce.

Serve warm or at room temperature with ice cream, fresh fruit, cakes, French toast (see page 180), or blinis (see page 178).

Tart Shell Pastry

YIELD

1, 11-INCH SPRINGFORM TART SHELL

1 vanilla bean (optional)

3 ounces (6 tablespoons) unsalted butter at room temperature

¾ cup confectioners' sugar, sifted

3 large egg yolks at room temperature

1¾ cups unbleached flour, sifted, divided

⅛ teaspoon sea salt

Unsalted butter for buttering the pan

Slit open the vanilla bean lengthwise and scrape the seeds out into the work bowl of a food processor or electric mixer. Add butter to the bowl and process until smooth. Add the sugar and process until a thick creamy paste forms. Add the egg yolks, process, scrape down the sides, and process again until smooth. Add 1½ cups flour and salt and process to form a dough. If the mixture remains creamy, work in the remaining flour, 2 tablespoons at a time. The dough should break up into small balls.

Scrape the dough out of the bowl onto a lightly dusted sheet of waxed paper. Lightly dust the top and flatten dough out into a disk. Wrap it airtight in plastic and refrigerate at least 1 hour, preferably longer, as long as overnight.

Thoroughly butter an 11-inch springform tart mold. Lightly flour the chilled pastry and roll it out between sheets of plastic wrap. Make the circle of pastry 1 inch larger than the diameter of the tart shell. Remove the top sheet of plastic and invert the dough into the mold. Press the dough into the mold carefully, pressing the edges of the dough against the side of the mold without stretching it. Gently peel off the remaining sheet of plastic. Trim the dough at the rim and prick it over the bottom. Cover and chill the lined mold at least 1 hour or tightly wrap and chill overnight.

Preheat oven to 375°F. Uncover and place the tart shell on a baking sheet and bake for 20 to 30 minutes, until the shell is lightly browned. Cool on a rack.

English Custard

YIELD
2½ CUPS

This custard formula is rich in egg yolks for extra body and color. You may wish to substitute 2 tablespoons of a fruit brandy or liqueur per cup of custard in place of vanilla if you want the custard to complement a specific fruit flavor.

2 cups half-and-half (light cream)

1 vanilla bean or 1 tablespoon vanilla paste

6 egg yolks

½ cup sugar

¼ teaspoon salt

Pour the cream into a heavy, non-reactive 1½-quart saucepan. Cut through the outer peel of the vanilla bean along its length with a paring knife. Scrape out the contents and add the seeds and pod to the cream. (If using vanilla paste, see the last paragraph.) Heat the cream to 180°F. This is the point when small bubbles appear at the edge of the pan and a skin forms over the cream.

While the cream is heating, whisk together egg yolks, sugar, and salt in a 2-quart bowl. Slowly pour 1 cup of the hot cream into the yolks, whisking vigorously. Return this mixture to the pan and heat, stirring constantly, until the custard coats the spoon and sides of the pan, about 170°F.

Strain the custard into a 1-quart measure and remove the vanilla bean pod or stir in the vanilla paste. Dot the custard's surface with the end of a stick of unsalted butter to prevent a skin from forming. Allow the custard to cool to room temperature, then cover tightly and refrigerate.

Jelly Roll Sponge Cake

YIELD
1 CAKE LAYER

A light, lemon-scented sponge cake is the perfect partner for a filling of rich strawberry preserves. Once rolled, this cake can be layered in a trifle (see page 211), or serve it in a deconstructed fashion, with two overlapping slices on a dessert plate, surrounded by custard and a fresh berry garnish.

5 large egg whites at room temperature (scant ¾ cup)

Pinch of salt

1 cup granulated sugar, divided

4 large egg yolks at room temperature

¾ cup flour, sifted before measuring

1 teaspoon grated lemon rind

Butter the bottom of a 10 × 15-inch sheet cake pan. Line it with waxed paper or parchment and butter the paper. Preheat oven to 350°F.

Beat the egg whites at medium speed in a mixer to soft peaks, adding a pinch of salt and ¼ cup sugar at the start. Add the remaining sugar slowly, continuing to beat as the whites gain body and flexibility. Lightly beat the yolks with a fork and fold them into the whites by hand. To fold, make a circular motion with a rubber spatula straight down into the center of the whites, then flat along the bottom, and finally up the sides, lifting whites to cover the added ingredient on the surface before turning the bowl and returning into the center to repeat until the addition is incorporated. Sift on the flour ¼ cup at a time, and gently fold it in, adding the grated lemon rind with the last of the flour.

Spoon the batter onto the cake sheet. Level it with a flat spatula. Bake for 20 minutes or until the cake is puffed and golden. Let the cake cool in its pan on a rack. Loosen the cake around the edges and turn it onto a strip of lightly oiled waxed paper 6 inches longer than the length of the pan. (If you are not filling this cake immediately, roll it up and store it in an airtight plastic bag in the refrigerator or freezer.)

Strawberry Jelly Roll

Spread the cooled cake with Strawberry Preserves (see pages 132, 141), and, using a long sheet of waxed paper under the cake, roll it up along the long edge. Wrap and refrigerate until serving time. Sprinkle with confectioners' sugar and cut into ¾-inch-thick slices. Serve two overlapping slices on each plate with a fresh strawberry garnish. Surround the slices with spoonfuls of English Custard (see page 215).

Crème Fraîche

This fermented heavy cream has a slightly tart flavor and the consistency of sour cream. The taste complements desserts made with fruit preserves, and its thick texture makes it an attractive garnish.

- **2** cups heavy whipping cream
- **2** tablespoons buttermilk, or plain yogurt with live cultures

Heat the cream to 100°F in a saucepan or microwave. Stir in the buttermilk or yogurt. Pour this mixture into a glass container with a tight lid. Keep the closed jar at room temperature, between 70° and 75°F, for 18 to 36 hours, until the cream has thickened noticeably. Refrigerate this cultured cream. It will continue to thicken, but more slowly in a colder temperature. Plan to use it within a month and stir it well each time before pouring.

A SEASONAL GUIDE TO

Fresh Fruits and Vegetables

FOR PRESERVING

ALMOST ALL THE FRUITS AND VEGETABLES THAT APPEAR IN *Artisanal Preserves* are now available year-round. While that limits the usefulness of a seasonal guide, the most important question for the fruit preserver has always been, "What's in season where I live?" Our ancestors wouldn't have had to ask this question.

The local farmers' market is a more reliable source than a supermarket where produce is shipped in from across the country. Frozen fruit is also less desirable, unless you have frozen it yourself and use it within the year.

This seasonal guide is still useful as a general reference and for its description of the best features of each fruit and vegetable used in *Artisanal Preserves*. It encourages shoppers to look at and evaluate the ripeness and general condition of their produce purchases. That said, I do describe the appearance of some fruits when they are under-ripe to encourage their use in small amounts (25%) to boost acid and pectin content.

The original resource for this listing in 1984 was the "Supply Guide" from the United Fresh Fruit and Vegetable Association, which indicated the availability of produce at wholesale markets rather than their harvest times. Italicized months indicate seasonal peaks. Many of the ripeness profiles that follow the dating were supplemented by information from *The Greengrocer* by Joe Carcione.

FRUITS

APPLES: All apples should be firm, well formed, glossy, and free of bruises and blemishes.

CORTLAND: September and October

GOLDEN DELICIOUS: year-round

GRANNY SMITH: all months except October

GREENING: October and November

JONATHAN: October to May

MACINTOSH: October to June

APRICOTS: late May through *June*, *July*, and August

Firm, golden, fuzzy fruits are best. A touch of pink blush indicates they are approaching full ripeness.

BLACKBERRIES: June, *July*, *August*, and September

Look for plump, dark blackberries with long caps packed with juicy lobes.

BLUEBERRIES: June, *July*, and *August*

Berries that are full, round, and firm with a dusty bloom are best. Include a few with a reddish tinge, which indicates they are slightly underripe and good for preserving.

BOYSENBERRIES: June, *July*, and *August*

These look like giant blackberries. Both whole berries and clustered lobes are larger and fuller. They are also quite fragile. Avoid baskets stained with juice. Store berries in a single layer and use them within two days.

CHERRIES, SOUR: June and *July*

Cherries should be bright red, slightly soft to the touch, and unblemished, with green stems attached.

CRABAPPLES: July and *August*

These miniature round apples can vary in color from bright orange-gold to dark red. Select large, unflawed ones from the tree rather than the ground if you are harvesting them yourself.

CRANBERRIES: *October, November*, and December

Color is not as good an indicator of quality as the condition of the fruit. Berries should be oval, firm, and bright, free of dents and soft spots.

CURRANTS, RED: July

These small berries should be a rich translucent red, perfectly round and on the stem.

FIGS, DRIED: year-round

Choose packages of golden Calimyrna or Kalamata figs that are gently firm but not hard or dry to the touch.

GRAPEFRUIT, PINK AND WHITE: October through March

This fruit should be round, firm, and heavy for its size. Peel is best when bright yellow and fine grained.

GRAPES, CONCORD: September and October

Good bunches will have well-developed side branches packed with dark, plump grapes that carry a natural dusty bloom.

KIWIFRUIT: California: October through May

This brown fuzzy fruit is ready for the preserving pot when it is still quite firm, yielding only slightly to gentle finger pressure.

LEMONS: year-round

Look for lemons that have a fine-grained skin and bright yellow color with a slightly greenish cast, which is a sign that they are barely ripe and wonderfully sour. Pick ones that are oval, firm, and feel heavy for their size.

LIMES: year-round

They should have the same features as lemons: good shape (in this case, round), bright color, no blemishes, and fine grain. A slightly yellowish tinge to the skin indicates ripeness, so choose the less ripe green ones.

NECTARINES: June through September

Nectarines should be bright yellow-gold with a fine red blush, which indicates they are just ripe. They will also be slightly soft along the seam of the fruit. Pick ones that are plump, well-formed, and free of bruises.

ORANGES, NAVEL: most available November through May

Color is not as good a guide to fruit maturity as the feel of the orange in your hand. You want it to be firm, round, and heavy for its size. The skin should be fine grained and free from mold and blemishes.

PEACHES: May, June, *July, August,* and September

Make sure the peaches you buy have a uniform yellow cast, which indicates they were not picked green. They should be firm but yield a bit to gentle pressure and give off a rich peach fragrance.

PEARS, BARTLETT: August through October

Pears are picked green, and you can purchase them at an early stage of ripening to let them slowly turn golden in your kitchen at room temperature. Use them when they have just turned yellow and before their tender skins give slightly to gentle pressure.

PINEAPPLES: year-round

The best signs of ripeness in a pineapple are a bright green crown and golden fruit color accompanied by a fragrant fruit scent. However, this ideally ripe pineapple is a rare find at the supermarket. You'll most likely have to sniff the scent at the stem end because the fruit will still be cold from refrigeration. If you find one that is fresh-looking and smelling, with only the lower third golden and the rest green, take it. The pineapple will continue to ripen satisfactorily in your kitchen. Do not purchase any fruit with brown leaves, soft spots, or a spoiled smell. Also note that a large pineapple has a higher percentage of flesh than a small one.

PLUMS, DAMSON: August

Damsons are small, plump, and tender spheres of deep purple.

PLUMS, ITALIAN: July, August, and *September*

Ripe Italian plums have a slightly hazy bloom over their dusty purple skins, and their plump oval lobes give under the thin skin. Some can be used for preserving when they are still rather firm and reddish in hue.

QUINCES: September, October, and November

The quince is a hard, knobby fruit when ripe. Only a gold cast over a green peel and a luscious apple aroma give any indication of ripeness. Cook them before they begin to shrivel at the stem end and soften to the touch.

RASPBERRIES, RED AND BLACK: *July*, August, and September (black in July only)

The caps of ripe raspberries easily slip off the stem. The lobes are firm, plump, and a richly colored shade of red or glossy blue-black. Do not buy boxes stained with fruit. Slide them out of their boxes onto a flat tray in one layer and use within a day or two.

RHUBARB: year-round but especially April and May

Although hothouse farming and summer gardens have made rhubarb available almost all year long, it still tastes best in the spring, when the first field crops are harvested. Deep red field rhubarb has a slightly tarter flavor than the lighter pink hothouse variety. Either is good for preserving as long as stalks are firm, moist, and free of cuts and bruises.

SERVICEBERRIES: June, *July*, and August

This is a crop you will have to pick yourself. The berries mature over the summer, becoming dark red and drier over time. They are best for preserving in late June and July. You may pluck them from the stem since they are small and not particularly juicy. Look for bright red color and round, plump shape.

STRAWBERRIES: April, May, and *June*

Strawberries do not have to be deeply red all over to be good for preserving. In fact, as many as 30 percent can be partly ripe. Small plump ones with bright green caps are preferred for preserves, though large berries may be halved or quartered, if necessary, for uniformity. You can store them as long as three days in a single layer in the refrigerator. Do not remove the caps or rinse them until you are ready to cook.

VEGETABLES

ONIONS: year-round

Look for firm young onions. Those that ripen early in the season are usually sweeter than the latecomers. (You will have to ask your produce manager about the source and season of the onions when you buy them.) Onion skins should be dry, the flesh firm. Stay away from onions whose neck ends are soft, discolored, or sprouting green stems.

PEPPERS, BELL AND JALAPEÑO: year-round

Bell and variety peppers can now be had many months of the year, though the jalapeño is more likely available at ethnic markets in the winter. Select peppers most brightly colored with a smooth, glossy surface. Turn them over in your hand to check for undesirable impact bruises and splits.

TOMATOES: Tomatoes taste best when used fresh from the garden in late summer: red, ripe, and luscious. The best time to select green ones is at the end of the season, before they succumb to frost.

ROUND VARIETIES: July, *August*, and *September*

ITALIAN PLUM: Late summer into fall

ZUCCHINI: year-round

Like the other vegetables listed here, zucchini is now available most months of the year. Small zucchini are preferred because they are the tenderest throughout. Select ones with a deep green skin, symmetrical oblong shape, and firmness at both ends.

Acknowledgments

I T'S BEEN MY PLEASURE to work with Agate Publishing again on this fourth edition of my preserving cookbook. Editor Amanda Gibson has helped meld new material into the existing manuscript and overseen the recipe updates. Jane Seibold has continued to refine *Artisanal Preserves*'s handbook format and selected a mouth-watering photo for the cover. Throughout the project, my daughter, Celia, has been an astute sounding board. Thanks to her skills as an illustrator, the technical drawings now have a uniformly professional look. I continue to be inspired on a daily basis by the support and tasting skills of my son, Benton, and his family.

INDEX